# Samuel de Champlain

## Contents

©1981, Fitzhenry and Whiteside Limited
150 Lesmill Road, Don Mills, Ontario M3B 2T5

*Editor* Rosalind Sharpe
*Designer* Sue Budd

Printed and bound in Canada by
T.H. Best and Company, Don Mills, Ontario

**The Canadians** a continuing series
*General Editor* Robert Read
*Series Editor* Rosalind Sharpe

CANADIAN CATALOGUING IN PUBLICATION DATA
Garrod, Stan.
  Samuel de Champlain

(The Canadians)
Bibliography: p. 64
Includes index.
ISBN 0-88902-683-1

1. Champlain, Samuel de, 1567-1635. 2. Explorers — France — Biography. 3. New France — Discovery and exploration. 4. Canada — Discovery and exploration — French. I. Title. II. Series.

FC332.G37    971.01'13'0924    C81-094406-5
F1030.1.G37

# Brouage Chapter 1

The stone walls of the sixteenth-century French town of Brouage rose directly from the sea. The waters of the Bay of Biscay that lapped at the walls brought prosperity to the small seaport, for the life of the community centred on the sea and on ships.

From the ramparts, or from the gun towers that defended the town, the children of Brouage could look far out to sea. Perched on the walls, they watched the movements of the sailing ships, some entering the port, others crossing the Bay of Biscay in the distance. From their lookouts, they could see French, English, or Spanish men-of-war pass on their way to the great battles that were so frequent at that time.

In more peaceful times, the children could watch the fishing boats moving in and out of the port. Many of the men of Brouage were fishermen, making their living in local waters. The young boys of the town sailed out with their fathers. They learned seaman's skills, the best way of mending nets and sails or splicing ropes, how to read the winds, the correct way to handle small boats in heavy seas.

There were always new things for them to learn. They watched eagerly for the arrival of merchant ships or larger fishing vessels in the port, for these boys knew and discussed ships just as young people today know different types of cars and airplanes. Many different ships from several countries could be seen tied up to great iron rings set in the stone walls of the town. There were Portuguese carracks, Flemish flyboats from the Spanish colonies in the Netherlands, and fast little pinnaces.

Of special interest were the boats that crossed the wide Atlantic Ocean, travelling thousands of kilometres to catch codfish off the Grand Banks of Newfoundland. They stopped at Brouage to take on salt, which was used to preserve fish, before heading west to the Grand Banks.

The boys of Brouage would watch as the fishermen readied their boats for the long ocean passage. They saw hulls being caulked, nets mended and stores taken on board in order to assure a safe and successful voyage. Often the fishermen would be drinking wine or brandy to help give them courage to face the dangerous crossing ahead. As they drank, they would tell stories of adventure on the high seas.

Sitting on the quayside, the boys listened spellbound as they heard of voyages across the stormy Atlantic. There were tales of courage and death in foreign lands, stories of the riches of far-off India and China. The sailors' words sketched wonderful scenes of great cities in Mexico and Peru, filled with gold and silver. They told of the strange and wondrous animals that supposedly lived in the seas and on distant shores. The fishermen spoke of the great sailors who had led the way across the oceans: Vasco da Gama, Columbus, Magellan, Cabot and Cartier.

Like the other boys of Brouage, Samuel de Champlain grew up with the magic spell of the sea all around him. His father and grandfather were both sea captains. The sea was his classroom and his playground.

Little is known about his family or his early life in Brouage. We don't even know for certain the year of his birth. From his writings, it has been suggested that he was born around 1570. Nothing is known of his parents except their names. In Champlain's marriage contract he gives these as Antoine de Complain and Marguerite Le Roy.

Champlain grew up at a time when most people could not read or write. Few of the children of Brouage went to school. They learned practical skills and had the lessons of hardship forced upon them by sieges and naval battles. Such lessons would have prepared Samuel de Champlain to be a soldier or a sailor. But, as he grew up, Champlain received a broader education than this. He could read and his journals show that he was able to write. He was also skilled in the mathematics of navigation, in mapmaking and in drawing. A French lawyer and playwright, Marc Lescarbot, who was with Champlain in Acadia, makes fun of the explorer's lack of Latin. This suggests that Champlain never went to school, since schools in those days almost always taught Latin and Greek. In all probability, Champlain learned his lessons at home. In later years, Champlain would combine this education with his experience at sea to

*A French merchant of the sixteenth century*

become the geographer, author and explorer that we remember today.

Champlain left no record of his experiences as a child or teenager in Brouage, but the history of the town tells us that in his youth he knew terror, hunger, hardship, war and the sight of death. Sixteenth-century France was torn apart by religious conflict. As opposing Catholic and Protestant forces struggled for control of the country, the strategic port of Brouage became a pawn in the contest. Again and again Brouage changed hands, as first Protestant and then Catholic factions besieged and overran the town.

Champlain's name, Samuel, suggests that he may have been born Protestant, for the Huguenots (French Protestants) often chose Old Testament names for their children, while the Catholics preferred the names of saints. We know that in adult life Champlain was a devout Catholic. If, during those years of strife and uncertainty, Champlain changed his religion, he was not alone. During one of the periods when the Huguenots controlled Brouage, Champlain caught his first glimpse of the Huguenot leader Henri of Navarre. Later, Henri would become a Catholic and ruler of France. Champlain would know and serve him well.

It is in this setting of protracted warfare that we come on the first historic record of Samuel de Champlain's career as a soldier and adventurer. As the war developed, it no longer pitted Protestant against Catholic. The Catholic forces led by Henri of Navarre, now king of France, fought against other Catholics for control of the kingdom. Henri's enemies were helped in the war by the Spanish. England, long an enemy of the French, nevertheless sent an army to Henri's aid.

Champlain joined the king's army in 1593, when he was in his twenties. In all probability, he had already spent several years at sea learning the sailor's trade. His first appointment was as a corporal in the quartermaster service. His leader was the Marshall d'Aumont, commander of the king's forces. D'Aumont was a strict chief, his army tightly disciplined. One day Champlain and the other soldiers watched as twenty-eight of their fellows were hanged for looting and disobeying orders. It was a situation that Champlain would recall as leader of the Quebec settlement many years later.

*Two mediaeval towers guard the entrance to the harbour of La Rochelle, a town close to Brouage on the Brittany coast. In the religious wars that tore sixteenth-century France apart, the two towns were sometimes friends and sometimes foes as they were seized and lost by rival armies.*

SHIPS & BOATS OF CHAMPLAIN'S TIME

*This pen-and-ink sketch by C.W. Jefferys shows the kind of craft Champlain must have watched from the walls of Brouage*

*Writing many years later, Champlain referred briefly to his childhood by the sea. In a letter to Marie de Medici, Queen Regent of France, he said, "The art of navigation from childhood has most of my life driven me to face the impetuous waves of the ocean."*

In the fall of 1594, d'Aumont's army was hard on the heels of the Spanish in northwest France. His soldiers forced a troop of some 400 retreating Spaniards on to a rocky promontory. The place was Crozon, which guards the southern entrance to the important harbour of Brest. Driven onto the lichen-covered rocks, the Spaniards stopped and turned. They used the rocks to build a fort which they defended heroically against repeated attacks.

Champlain fought alongside the English forces in the final assault on Crozon on November 7, 1594. The English soldiers were led by Sir Martin Frobisher, an early explorer of the Canadian arctic. Frobisher had been one of the first to seek the Northwest Passage, a water route around the top of North America to China. Champlain would embark on a similar search a few years later. Did Champlain know of the English leader and his earlier adventures at this time? We have no way of knowing, but later Champlain would praise the efforts of Frobisher as one who marked the way for the exploration of Canada.

For the moment, however, Champlain's thoughts must have been entirely given to the task at hand. The Spanish defended themselves well, raining fire on the attackers. In the final assault, many French and English soldiers died before the fort was reached and taken. One of the dead was Frobisher, who was killed as he stormed the fort. Of the 401 Spaniards who had defended Crozon, only eleven were still alive, nine of them badly wounded. Nearly 3000 French and English soldiers had been lost in the battle.

As the war dragged on through 1595, Marshal d'Aumont died, killed at the age of seventy-three while attempting to capture a castle as a favour to a countess with whom he had fallen in love. He was replaced as commander by d'Epinay Saint-Luc, the former governor of Brouage. D'Epinay appears to have shown favour to his fellow townsman. Champlain served him as *maréchal de logis*, the officer in charge of finding accommodation for the soldiers. The experience of trying to keep an army supplied and housed under the fearful conditions of the war in Brittany proved useful to Champlain years later, when he was establishing settlements at Port Royal and Quebec.

He served his commander and king well. When the war ended with complete victory for the royal armies, he was left with good connections. These eventually brought him a pension from King Henri and royal friendship, supportive of his efforts in Canada.

The young officer who stood to attention as Henri IV reviewed his victorious troops in May 1598 had been toughened by five years of long, cruel war. He had learned how to take care of himself and how to take responsibility for those who served under him. He had learned old soldiers' tricks for staying comfortable in rain or snow, or for finding something to eat when no food was to be had. He had learned to kill, and to live with death and suffering. It was a good apprenticeship for service in a far-off land that could be no more savage than war-torn Brittany.

Following the review, the king heard a *Te Deum* sung in Rennes Cathedral to honour the victory, and then enjoyed five days of celebration. Wine flowed, heroic songs were sung, and stories of bravery, hardship, and death were told and told again until the wine ran out. At the end of the five days, the soldiers were given their separation pay and sent their own ways. Samuel de Champlain was out of work.

# Chapter 2 The Old World And The New

Seeing myself, without work or any other thing to do, I made up my mind that I would not remain idle. I set about finding some means of making a voyage to Spain, and, being there, to make and cultivate useful friends. By their influence, I intended to ship out in one of the vessels sent every year by the king of Spain to the West Indies. In doing so, I wished to inform myself of things not yet seen by any Frenchman, because they have not had free access to the area. And so, on my return, I would make a truthful report of them to His Majesty.

With these words Samuel de Champlain began a report, written early in 1603, telling the king of his first journey across the Atlantic. It was a trip that took him, not to Canada, but to Mexico and the West Indies.

We can imagine Champlain after the end of the war in Brittany. Still a young man and filled with a strong desire for adventure, he was restless and eager to be on the move again. He saw his opportunity in the plan to return Spanish troops to the homeland after their defeat in Brittany. The young officer made his way across Brittany to the port of Blavet on the south coast. There, the Spanish soldiers were being held until their return to Spain under the terms of the treaty that ended the war.

In Blavet, Champlain met up with an uncle, Guillaume Allene, called Captain Provençal after his native region. In his report, Champlain tells us that his uncle was "one of the great seamen of France. And, in that status he had been employed by the king of Spain as a pilot-general in his navy." Captain Provençal had hired his ship, the *Saint-Julien*, to the Spanish. The *Saint-Julien* was a sturdy vessel that had previously been used in the Newfoundland fishing trade. Allene invited his nephew to travel as his guest to Spain. They set sail from France on September 9, 1598. Champlain learned how to handle a large sailing vessel, and listened as members of the *Saint-Julien's* crew talked of their voyages to Newfoundland.

After a difficult crossing of the Bay of Biscay the fleet made anchor at the Spanish port of Cadiz. Champlain spent the next four months in Spain, exploring Cadiz and the neighbouring city of Seville, sketching and drawing his first crude maps of the places he visited, and making good his intention to "cultivate useful friends."

Soon after arriving in Cadiz and depositing their companies of Spanish prisoners-of-war on Spanish soil, the French ships were sent back to France. The speed and seaworthiness of the *Saint-Julien*, however, attracted the attention of a Spanish admiral, Don Francisco Coloma. Coloma was in command of a convoy about to leave for the Spanish colonies; he decided to charter the *Saint-Julien* for the voyage. Captain Provençal, the ship's master, had other duties that called him back to France. He persuaded Coloma to allow Champlain to accompany the ship to the New World in his place.

Spain's colonies in America depended on the mother country for many of the manufactured goods they needed. In return, the Spaniards obtained rich amounts of gold, silver, dyes and other valuable commodities from the colonies. This trade was closely guarded against foreign intrusions. All the goods had to travel in Spanish ships; every year a great fleet set out from Spain for the Indies, returning with valuable cargos. The fleets were tempting targets for English, French and Dutch pirates.

Coloma's fleet left Sanlucar de Barrameda at the mouth of the Guadalquivir River on February 3, 1599. The crossing followed the usual route of the day, staying off the coast of Africa as far as the Canary Islands, bearing south and west to the sixteenth parallel of latitude, then sailing due west. Two months and six days after the fleet left Sanlucar, Champlain first saw land in the Americas: they had reached the island of Deseada in the West Indies, just east of Guadeloupe. Champlain must have marvelled at the skill of the fleet's navigator who, throughout all the weeks at sea, had kept them right on course. When the fleet stopped for supplies in Guadeloupe, Champlain saw native Americans for the first time. The sailors returned to their ships with loads of fresh fruit, meat and water. "How good it tasted," wrote Champlain, showing uncharacteristic enthusiasm for worldly pleasures.

After passing through the Virgin Islands, Champlain visited Puerto Rico. The fleet dropped anchor in the fine harbour of San Juan where, according to Champlain's reports, they found the fort and town in ruins. San Juan, an important centre of Spanish trade in the Indies, had been ransacked by the English in June, 1598. The Duke of Cumberland had captured the port, taking cargos of hides, sugar and ginger as prizes. But the English had only occupied the town; they had not destroyed it. They had held it until yellow fever and dysentery drove them out in November of the same year. Why Champlain should exaggerate the damage is not clear. Perhaps he wanted to convince the king of the fierceness with which the English were competing with the Spanish for the riches of the New World. He hoped to encourage the French to do the same.

Champlain stayed a month in Puerto Rico, sketching trees and plants and especially the lush tropical fruits. At the end of that time the Spanish fleet divided into three groups. One sailed for the northeast coast of South America, another group headed for Portobello carrying goods for Panama and Peru, and three galleons headed for Mexico, taking Champlain with them.

The ships docked at San Juan de Ulua, the modern port of Vera Cruz. San Juan was the chief port of New Spain, the most important of the American colonies.

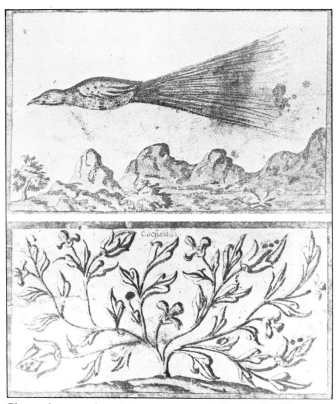

*Champlain often sketched the strange things he saw and heard about on his travels. His drawings, like his accounts, reflect his lively interest in unfamiliar places and lifestyles. These sketches show some of the unusual plants he saw in South America and also the curious Quetzal bird, which, according to Champlain, "spends all of its time in the air and never comes to earth until it falls dead. It is about the size of a sparrow, with a tail like an egret. It has no feet. . . . As I say, I saw only one of these creatures."*

*Champlain also records as a fact the presence of dragons in Mexico.*

Champlain explored the area around San Juan for two weeks, then set off across the mountains for Mexico City. He passed through great forests filled with brightly coloured tropical birds. He also saw farms and great herds of cattle, signs of settlement which told him the Spaniards were there to stay.

Champlain was impressed by Mexico City. In his report he writes, "I was amazed by the beauty of the temples, palaces, and great houses; I had not thought they would be so magnificent. The streets are so well laid-out, with fine big shops filled with goods of all kinds. My guess is that there are 12 000-15 000 Spaniards in the city, 75 000-80 000 Indians, all Christians, and many thousands of Negro slaves." The riches of Mexico greatly impressed Champlain, as did the fertile lands and fine farms and ranches.

Champlain was moved by the condition of the Indians. His report is critical of the Inquisition in New Spain, which "condemned so many of the natives to slavery or death that the very telling of it brings tears to one's eyes." Champlain felt that more gentle measures were needed to bring native peoples to a "love of God and a belief in His Holy Church." Champlain would remember the Mexicans' experiences with Christianity in his attempts to convert the native peoples of New France.

From Mexico, Champlain travelled to Portobello in Panama. He found Panama to be a great contrast to Mexico, for its soil was poor and its climate unhealthy. But the harbours were good, and Champlain took pains to point out in his report that all the gold and silver of Peru passed through Portobello. To encourage further royal support, he noted that the port was poorly guarded and could easily be taken. Crossing the narrow isthmus of Panama, Champlain had his first glimpse of the Pacific Ocean; beyond the horizon lay China. He would spend the rest of his life trying to reach the Pacific for the second time. In his report, he suggests the possibility of building a canal from the Atlantic to the Pacific across the isthmus. The idea was not a new one, having been put forward as early as 1534 when the Spanish king, Carlos V, set up a commission to investigate the possibility; but it does show where Champlain's dreams and vision were focused.

Returning to San Juan de Ulua, Champlain rejoined the Spanish fleet. He spent several months more in the Indies, visiting Havana and, by his account, Cartagena in Colombia, far to the south. The fleet sailed back to Spain from Havana early in 1601.

In 1603, some time after his return, Champlain wrote his report of the journey for the king. Part of the purpose of the report was to draw attention to himself, to obtain royal support for further adventures. The original is a strikingly beautiful little book, including sixty-two water-colour maps and illustrations. They show remarkable scenes of life in the Spanish Indies: tropical trees and plants, fantastic animals, silver mines, the burning of Indians by the Inquisition in Mexico. The book seems to have had the desired effect. Despite criticism from rivals at court, Champlain succeeded in winning the favour of the king whose entry into Brouage he had watched nearly thirty years before. He was given a royal pension, and was appointed to the king's service.

# New France Chapter 3

Barefoot, Samuel de Champlain walked toward the old stone church of Notre-Dame-de-Grâce. With him were François Pont-Gravé and the crew of his ship, the *Bonne Renommeé*, which was about to carry Champlain on his first trip to what is now Canada. Before sailing, the French seamen traditionally made this barefoot pilgrimage to the church on the cliff overlooking the port of Honfleur. Should he return safely from across the Atlantic, Champlain would once again leave his boots at home and walk to the church to give thanks.

The *Bonne Renommeé* sailed for Canada on March 15, 1603. She was part of a small fur-trading fleet of three ships put together by an old friend of Champlain, Aymar de Chastes, governor of Dieppe. After this first exploratory trip, de Chastes hoped to lead a band of colonists to settle in the New World. He had invited Champlain to join the exploratory party. Champlain quickly agreed; it was just the chance he had been waiting for. With the king's permission, he hastened to Honfleur.

Champlain's journal of the trip tells us that it was a rough crossing. The ships battled storm after storm, and while they were still 400 km off the coast of North America they had to swing south to avoid ice.

Champlain notes that they crossed the Grand Banks of Newfoundland on May 2. Four days later, through thick fog, he could hear surf breaking on a nearby shore. His first sight of land was Cape St. Mary on the southeast coast of Newfoundland. On May 20, the ships sighted Anticosti Island and entered the St. Lawrence River. The next day, Champlain saw for the first time the steep face of Cape Gaspé, which would, over the years, become a familiar landmark for him. The ships made their way up the south shore of the river to Bic, then crossed to Tadoussac on the north side. On May 26, the ships dropped anchor in the harbour at Tadoussac, the first French fur-trading post in Canada.

During the voyage, Champlain had ample opportunity to learn something about the country to which he was headed. Captain Pont Gravé, a stout, hearty man, close to fifty, had made several trading trips to the St. Lawrence. His sense of humour eased difficult situations at sea; his strong voice boomed out across the water to greet fishing boats; he often treated the crew to a lusty version of some old Breton song. Champlain liked the captain immediately and the two men became friends. It was the beginning of a partnership that would last nearly thirty years.

Two other passengers on the crossing could tell Champlain even more about the life in the New World. They were Montagnais Indians whom Pont-Gravé had picked up at Tadoussac on an earlier voyage. He had brought them back to France to be trained as interpreters. They were treated royally while in France, even meeting the king himself. Pont-Gravé intended to use the Montagnais natives as more than mere interpreters; they were to reassure their people of the good intentions of the French. In this way, he hoped to establish good relations between the traders and the native people.

Champlain first set foot on the soil of Canada on May 27, 1603. He and Pont-Gravé came ashore at Cape St. Matthew near Tadoussac to find themselves in the midst of a *tabagie* or Indian celebration. As they came ashore, accompanied by the two young Indian interpreters, they saw many birch-bark canoes pulled up on the beach. In the lodge of the *sagamore*, or chief, they found a company of between eighty and one hundred Montagnais celebrating a victory over the Iroquois. The Indians were eager to hear what the newcomers had to say. Champlain and Pont-Gravé were given places of honour beside the *sagamore*.

The interpreters who had just returned from France spoke first, describing their experiences in France, the castles and palaces they had seen, the French people and their way of life. We can get some sense of how the interpreters must have struggled to find words to describe their experiences from the report of a later missionary who spoke the Indian language. He heard a native, just returned from Europe, speak of "cabins pulled by moose." The Indian was trying to describe a horse-drawn carriage to people who had never seen such a thing. The interpreters brought greetings from the king of France and news of the plans to establish settlements in Canada. If necessary, they said, the French would help them defeat their enemies, the Iroquois. Champlain did not know it at the time, but this promise would bring him many problems in the future.

The *sagamore* paid close attention to all that was said. Then, still without speaking, he began to smoke his pipe. After he had smoked for some time, he passed the pipe to Pont-Gravé, then to Champlain and several nearby chiefs of lesser rank. When this brief ceremony was over he began to speak, pausing dramatically to emphasize important points.

The chief welcomed the French visitors, saying the Montagnais felt that the king of France was a friend. Champlain reports that the gathering agreed with these remarks, saying *"ho, ho, ho,"* that is, "yes, yes, yes," with great enthusiasm. The chief went on to say he was pleased that the French were going to settle in Canada and help defeat the Iroquois. Speaking of the benefits he expected to receive from the French, the Indian leader said that his people had no better friends in all the world. As events would later prove, he was backing the wrong side.

After staying two weeks with the Montagnais at Tadoussac, Champlain began his exploration of the surrounding region. First he travelled north along the Saguenay River for about 60 km. He found the landscape upstream from Tadoussac to be "wild and forbidding." He did not travel very far north of the St. Lawrence, but from the native people he learned much about the region and the trading methods of its inhabitants. The Indians also told him of a great salt sea, far to the north of the Saguenay. Champlain believed this would prove to be "part of the Atlantic Ocean, extending northward into the heart of the continent." He was right: six years later it was explored, and named Hudson Bay, by Henry Hudson.

On June 18, returning from the Saguenay, Champlain set out to explore the St. Lawrence River upstream from Tadoussac. He travelled in a small sailing vessel, a pinnace that had crossed the Atlantic on the deck of the *Bonne Renommée*. It was a familiar trip for Pont-Gravé, who commanded the pinnace, but one filled with a thousand new experiences for Champlain. He

*King Henri IV of France was chief sponsor of Champlain's voyages*

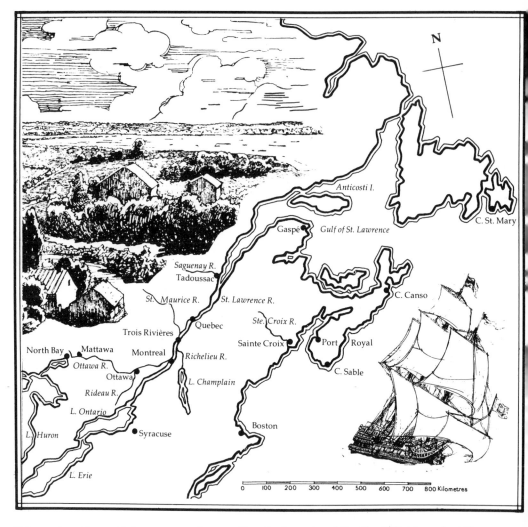

*This map shows the area that was explored by Champlain, and many of the settlements he visited or helped establish.*

was charmed by the beauty of the Ile d'Orléans, but the Montmorency Falls failed to impress him. The countryside he found "green and pleasant" but spoiled by the presence of mountains in the distance.

Four days out of Tadoussac, they dropped anchor at a point where the St. Lawrence narrows sharply. To the north there was a high point of land, dropping off steeply to the river on both sides. This was Champlain's first view of Quebec. His initial impressions were favourable:

The land is level and fertile, covered with oak, cypress, birch, fir and aspen. There are many grape vines and wild fruit trees. This makes me think that if the soil were cultivated, it would bear as richly as the land of France.

Already, the images of settlement, of French farms and homes at Quebec, were in Champlain's mind.

Navigation of the St. Lawrence became more difficult west of Quebec, for the way was obstructed by shallows, sandbars, and rapids. Champlain took careful notes of the best route to follow, already planning to revisit this region. Again, his journal shows that he was very impressed by the rich and fertile lands through which the river ran, and his thoughts turned to the possibility of French ploughs breaking the soil of the lands along the St. Lawrence. He was immediately struck by the possibilities Trois Rivières offered for settlement. He noted that it could be easily defended and would allow the French a means of protecting the Huron against Iroquois attack. The rivers would allow easy access for native traders. He tried to explore the St. Maurice in a skiff, but was driven back by the current.

Continuing up the St. Lawrence west of the Iroquois River, the St. Lawrence valley became flatter and much wider. The land, still rich and fertile, was covered by thick vegetation. Champlain spotted many different fruits and berries growing in profusion. The forests were filled with game, supplying the native people with both food and furs.

The Lachine Rapids blocked their progress westward through an area of many small islands, so, on July 2, the pinnace's anchor was dropped in the shelter of an island near the north shore of the river. They had reached the site of the modern city of Montreal, which Cartier had visited in 1535. The village of Hochelaga, where the Huron had entertained Cartier, was gone, the Huron having been driven westward by the Iroquois. No natives appeared to greet Champlain's party. The Huron's bark longhouses had fallen into decay and were covered with vines and brambles.

Champlain was impressed by the force and extent of the Lachine Rapids. He realized that to explore further up the river he would have to use Indian canoes, for the French boats were too heavy to portage around obstacles. Champlain was quickly learning the ways of this new land. He was learning, too, of the world beyond the rapids. His native companions told him of large bodies of water lying to the west. One, they suggested, was a great sea where the water never froze. This fired

*Title page of the first edition of Champlain's book,* Of the Savages, *which tells the story of his first voyage to New France*

*Champlain's works have been collected, reprinted and translated by the Champlain Society.*

Champlain's imagination. Could they be that close to the Pacific? A careful geographer, Champlain noted in his journal, "We should not take this for granted without good reason, but it does seem likely." Other Indians they met confirmed that a large body of water did indeed lie to the west. From their information Champlain calculated that "the great salt sea" lay about 2000 km from the rapids which had blocked his progress. He concluded: "If the sun sets where they say it does, it must be the Pacific Ocean." As he would later discover, the natives were in fact telling him of the Great Lakes. For the moment, however, he felt he was within reach of the fabled "passage to Cathay" that Frobisher and others had searched for in vain.

Pont-Gravé and Champlain returned to Tadoussac and met up once again with the Montagnais. The French traded for beaver and marten pelts, watched a war dance, and dried codfish in the sun for the return voyage.

The trip back to France took the *Bonne Renommée* along the St. Lawrence and out past Cape Breton Island. Along the river, Champlain learned of native copper mined by the Indians. In the account of the trip he published a few months after his return to France, he accurately reports the presence of this resource. Unlike other explorers, he did not intend to spread exaggerated rumours of gold, silver and precious jewels to be found in the New World. Yet in the same account he reports, as fact, tales the Micmac Indians told him of Gougou, a gigantic monster woman who kept her victims in her pocket before eating them. Whether Champlain believed the stories about Gougou or not, his account of her certainly must have helped the sales of his journal, *Of the Savages, or the Voyage of Samuel Champlain of Brouage to New France in the Year 1603.*

It was a deeply satisfied Champlain who once again made the barefoot pilgrimage to the church overlooking Honfleur's Harbour. It had been a safe and profitable trip. The furs and dried codfish loaded at Tadoussac had brought a good return when sold in France. More important to Champlain, he had learned a great deal about New France. He was convinced that a great settlement could be created there, with rich farms and prosperous towns. He was eager to return.

# The Winter Lasts Six Months! Chapter 4

Champlain returned to France to find that during his
absence his friend and patron, Aymar de Chastes, had
died. Now committed to further exploration of Canada,
Champlain had to seek support elsewhere. He
approached the king, telling him that the St. Lawrence
River could be a route to the Pacific and the riches of
Cathay. He spoke with great enthusiasm about the fertile
soils of the great river valley and outlined in persuasive
terms his own vision of a French settlement on the St.
Lawrence.

The king was already thinking along the same lines.
He had granted the Sieur de Monts, an investor in de
Chastes' project, a ten-year monopoly on the fur trade in
Canada. In return, de Monts was expected to establish
French royal authority over the territories in the New
World. He was instructed to make peace with the
Indians living there, to bring Christianity to them, to
colonize the new lands, and to seek mines of precious
metals such as silver and gold.

King Henri put Champlain in touch with de Monts, a
Huguenot who came from Champlain's own region of
France. De Monts was impressed both by Champlain's
knowledge of New France and by his strength of
character. He quickly invited the explorer to join his
expedition, due to leave early in 1604. Champlain,
always a prudent and cautious man, first sought the
king's permission to make the trip. Royal approval was
quickly given. The king asked only that Champlain make
a faithful report to him of all that he saw and discovered
in the New World.

Champlain must have felt quite at home when, on
March 7, 1604, after the ritual barefoot pilgrimage, he set
sail from Honfleur for his second voyage to New France.
One of the ships in the expedition was the *Bonne
Renommée,* a ship Champlain knew and trusted. His
good friend Captain Pont-Gravé was one of the skippers.

The expedition of 1604 was much larger than the one

*Jacques Cartier*

of a year earlier. On board the two ships were 120 colonists, including workmen, carpenters and stone masons. There were also soldiers, Swiss mercenaries, who were to guard against attack and enforce de Monts' monopoly. Surgeons had been brought along to care for the colonists' health through the harsh North American winter, and there were a Roman Catholic priest and a Huguenot minister to tend to their spiritual needs. The expedition's sponsor, the Sieur de Monts, came along, as did another nobleman, Jean de Biencourt, Seigneur de Poutrincourt. Poutrincourt hoped to establish a feudal estate for his family in the wilds of New France. The two ships carrying the colonists were joined by two fur-trading vessels and a whaling ship.

The craft planned to rendezvous at Cape Canso on the east coast of Nova Scotia. From there, they would proceed together to the St. Lawrence River. Champlain was eager to return to the upper river and push on beyond the point where he had turned back the previous year. He was certain that "the great salt sea" and China lay within his reach, and he wanted to find the route.

On the way across the Atlantic, de Monts changed his plans. He decided that the expedition would seek a site for colonization farther south, on the Atlantic Coast. Champlain felt that de Monts was afraid to defend his fur monopoly against the French fur traders already on the St. Lawrence. Others have suggested that de Monts, who had read of Cartier's tragic winter at Quebec, was even more afraid of the harsh Canadian winter. Champlain was bitterly disappointed but had no choice but to go along with his leader's decision.

After spending a week along the Nova Scotia coast the colonists turned south, searching for a place to set up temporary headquarters. On their way they came across a ship from Le Havre, trading furs in defiance of de Monts' monopoly. De Monts was furious at the violation of his right to be the only legal trader for furs. He ordered the ship's guns to be run out and seized the intruding ship and its captain.

The ship carrying Champlain and de Monts had been separated from Pont-Gravé and the *Bonne Renommée* during the stormy Atlantic crossing. While waiting for his old friend to arrive, Champlain spent three weeks exploring the coast of Nova Scotia and the waters of the

Bay of Fundy. In one spot he found a wooden cross, covered with moss. Europeans evidently had visited the area long before Champlain, judging from the decayed condition of the cross.

On his return he found the men rebellious and ready to return to France. They had used up most of the supplies, including those of the captured ship. Fortunately, Pont-Gravé soon arrived. He had been delayed by the task of seizing four Basque trading ships and their valuable cargos of furs. Champlain made sure that the new supplies Pont-Gravé brought were used prudently.

It was now the second week in June. The time had come to find a place to settle for the winter. De Monts and Champlain set out to explore the Bay of Fundy in more detail, hoping to find a suitable spot. One of the first places they examined was the beautiful natural harbour of the Annapolis Basin. The seamen on board de Monts' ship shouted out with delight at the beauty of the harbour. Champlain estimated that the basin could hold two thousand ships riding at anchor. He named the place Port Royal, a name it would bear as long as there were French in Acadia. No one was more impressed by Port Royal than the Sieur de Poutrincourt, who expressed a wish to settle there with his family. Exercising his power as lord of New France, de Monts made out a deed giving Poutrincourt the lands around Port Royal.

De Monts was unsure about the Port Royal site. He decided to keep on looking for a better place for the winter camp. After reaching the head of the Bay of Fundy, the party turned south along the coast of New Brunswick. On June 24, St. John the Baptist Day, they entered a good harbour at the mouth of a river that was wide and deep. De Monts named the place after St. John, whose name it bears today as the major city of New Brunswick. Again, de Monts was not certain he had found the best spot to pass the coming winter. The search was resumed and the ship headed south, sailing through island-dotted coastal waters.

At Passamaquoddy Bay the ship entered a broad tidal estuary, the mouth of the Ste. Croix River. Travelling a few kilometres upriver, de Monts spotted a peaceful little island, a welcome sight in the warm sun of a summer afternoon. He decided that this was the place for his headquarters in the New World. It was a fateful choice; the serenity of the sunlit island gave no hint of the horrors of the winter to follow.

Champlain agreed with de Monts' decision:

This place we considered the best we had seen, both on account of its location in such fine country and for the contact we hoped to make with the natives of the coast and the interior, since we were in their midst. In time we hope to pacify them, to end the wars they fight with each other, so that we may get them to serve us and also convert them to the Catholic faith.

The small company of explorers gave no thought to the cold winds of winter while they worked through the hot summer days to build a settlement on Ile Ste. Croix.

*This is Champlain's map of the Annapolis Basin, showing the settlement which was founded at Port Royal after the first disastrous winter at Ste. Croix. Comparison with a modern atlas will show how accurate this early seventeenth-century map is.*

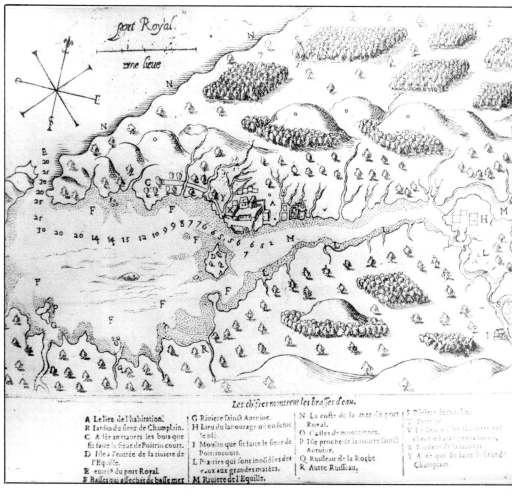

port Royal.

une lieue

Les chiffres monstrent les brasses d'eau.

A Le lieu de l'habitation.
B Jardin du sieur de Champlain.
C Allée au trauers les bois que fit faire le sieur de Poitrincourt.
D Isle a l'entrée de la riuiere de l'Equille.
E entrée du port Royal.
F Basses qui assechent de basse mer.
G Riuiere sainct Antoine.
H Lieu du labourage où on seme le blé.
I Moulin que fit faire le sieur de Poitrincourt.
L Prairies qui sont innondées des eaux aux grandes marées.
M Riuiere de l'Equille.
N La coste de la mer du port Royal.
O Costes de montaignes.
P Isle proche de la riuiere sainct Antoine.
Q Ruisseau de la Roche.
R Autre Ruisseau,
S Prairies du moulin.
T Petit lac.
V Le lieu où les sauuages pesehent le hareng en la saison.
X Ruisseau de la riuiere.
Y Allée que fit faire le sieur de Champlain.

Indeed, many of them must have longed for cooler days to come as they laboured under the burning sun. Black flies and mosquitoes swarmed around their heads. Insect bites left their faces so swollen that some of the men could hardly see.

The trees of the island were cut down to build a fortified village. The first task was to construct a barricade and set the cannon in place. Guns from the ship were brought ashore and placed facing south, to defend against attack from the sea. Their security assured, the colonists set about clearing ground and putting up buildings in which to spend the winter. Besides accommodation for the men, a storehouse, chapel, kitchen, forge, baker's oven, and handmill for grinding grain were built.

*Some of the features noted in the key to the map opposite are: A. the habitation;   B. Champlain's garden;   H. cornfields;   I. water mill;   L. salt marshes which flood at high tide (these marshes were later reclaimed by French settlers, who built dams to keep out the sea, and cultivated the fertile land that was exposed);   V. site where the natives catch fish.*

De Monts was well prepared for constructing his first home in the New World. The settlement at Ste. Croix may have been the first prefabricated town in North America: sawn timbers, doors, windows and furnishings were carried from France in the ships' holds. The result, as we can see from Champlain's sketches of the settlement, was a far cry from a simple log shelter. The buildings were substantial and well built. Two hundred years later, their remains could still be seen.

Fields were cleared and planted, both on the island and along the riverbanks on the mainland. Every man had his own garden plot. The rye they sowed thrived, but most of the other shoots, planted late in the season, withered in the summer sun. There was no supply of fresh water, so the settlers had to rely on occasional rainstorms.

While his companions laboured on the land, Champlain again took to the sea to explore the Bay of Fundy. He was searching, as he had been on his first trip around the bay, for a legendary copper mine which supposedly lay at the head of the Bay of Fundy. Despite his persistence, Champlain discovered nothing more than a few thin seams of native copper.

September found Champlain exploring again, this time to the southwest of Ste. Croix, following the rocky and foggy coast of Maine. He travelled in a small boat equipped with both sails and oars, ideal for exploring and mapping the coast. With him were twelve soldiers, and two natives who served as guides and ambassadors.

Champlain was visiting these shores as both a geographer and as a businessman. He noted the safe and sheltered harbours and traded with the Indians he met. Travelling with only a few armed men, Champlain approached the natives peacefully. He waited patiently when contact was made, giving the natives time to feel safe in coming to him. His peaceful approach overcame the Indians' initial shyness and distrust. The friendship he established between the French and the Indians in Acadia continued unbroken as long as the French remained there.

Aware that winter was fast approaching, Champlain returned to the Ste. Croix base on October 2, 1604. Four days later, the first snow fell. That year, winter set in very early and very hard. Instead of protecting the colonists, the island trapped them. As winter settled in, winds from the north and the west blew fiercely, wailing eerily through the logs and timbers of the houses. The search for building materials had stripped away the trees from the island, leaving no protection against the biting gales. With the trees gone, there was soon no firewood to keep the settlers warm. Great cakes of ice appeared in the river; the grinding pack ice kept the colonists from crossing the 800 m of river to reach the mainland. They were cut off from supplies of water, wood and fresh meat.

Soon snow covered the island. It lay until the end of April, steadily increasing to a depth of 100 cm or more. The men drank melted snow and ate cold salted meat and frozen vegetables. All their beverages froze except the Spanish wine. Rations of frozen apple cider were served by weight. Few meals were cooked, for firewood was too precious to permit much cooking. Weakened by cold and hunger, the settlers were struck by disease. Champlain records the terrible plight of those suffering from the incurable, unknown illness:

There was found in the mouths of those who had it, large pieces of rotting flesh. This increased so greatly that they could scarcely eat anything except in liquid form. Their teeth barely were held in place and could be pulled out with the fingers without causing pain. Their mouths bled. Afterwards, they were taken with great pains in their arms and legs. They became swollen and covered with spots like flea-bites. They could not walk, so great was the pain . . . They could not stand up without fainting dead away. Of seventy-nine of us, thirty-five died, and more than twenty were close to death. Even those who kept well complained of minor pains and shortness of breath.

Champlain's scientific curiosity led him to dissect several of the dead in an attempt to find the cause of the disease. He writes a horrible description of the state of their internal organs. Today we know that the colonists were suffering from scurvy, caused by a lack of vitamin C.

For the weakened survivors at Ste. Croix the only cure was the coming of spring. In March local Indians appeared, trading fresh meat for trinkets. Green shoots emerged through the snow and were eagerly devoured by the hungry men. With the spring thaw, Champlain and the others eagerly awaited the arrival of Pont-Gravé from France with a shipload of supplies.

Champlain himself appears to have been little affected by the outbreak of scurvy that nearly wiped out the colony. He and a few others who had been in good physical condition to begin with remained healthy and active. His attitude would not let him slip into the apathy and despair which overtook so many of the men. His harsh introduction to winters in the New World did not reduce his interest in colonization but, as he warned in his journal, "It is impossible to know this country without having wintered there. On arriving in summer everything is very pleasant . . . *But winter in this country lasts six months.*" Ironically, most winters along the

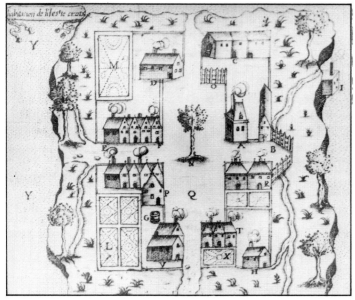

*Champlain's drawing of the Ste.-Croix settlement Key: A. Sieur de Mont's lodging; B. covered gallery; C. storehouse; D. barracks for Swiss soldiers; E. forge; F. carpenter's lodging; G. well; H. bread oven; I. (overhanging the river) kitchen; L,M. gardens; P. Champlain's and Champdoré's lodging.*

Atlantic coast are mild. Had it been a normal winter for the area, the colonists could have fished and hunted without difficulty, perhaps avoiding scurvy entirely.

The snows of winter slowly gave way to spring, but still there was no sign of Pont-Gravé. De Monts, Champlain and the other survivors prepared to abandon the colony. It was decided they should take the pinnaces and set out for the Gulf of St. Lawrence, where they could be rescued by passing fishermen. The date of departure was set for the end of June.

On the evening of June 15, Champlain was taking his turn as sentry. Through the dusk he caught sight of a sail. It was Pont-Gravé in a small shallop, making his way toward the island. His ship was anchored out in the estuary. His arrival brought new life and hope to the venture. De Monts decided not to abandon the scheme, but to move the colony to a more healthy spot in a milder climate.

Champlain set out to explore the coast to the south of the island. This time he was second in command, for De Monts had decided to lead the search for a new site himself. Champlain carefully recorded the details of the coast, mapping the important harbours they found. The voyage took them as far south as Boston Harbour at the mouth of the Charles River. On their way they visited Plymouth, where the Pilgrims would settle a few years later, and Nantucket. Champlain's maps of both these harbours have survived and are amazingly accurate, given the little time and crude tools he had to make them.

Less than fifty years later these harbours would be the heart of the prosperous and fast-growing New England colonies, the base from which the English would eventually drive the French from North America. Surprisingly, de Monts decided that none of these spots was suitable for his colony. He ordered the ship to return to Ile Ste. Croix.

De Monts had decided to move the colony to Port Royal on the Annapolis Basin. Bit by bit the tools, fitted timbers, doors and windows were removed from the buildings, loaded on board ship and carried across the Bay of Fundy. Ste. Croix, the first European colony in North America north of the Carolinas, was abandoned. Today, the island marks the boundary between the United States and Canada along the Ste. Croix River.

# The Order Of Chapter 5
# Good Cheer

At Port Royal, de Monts' colonists set about building a small fortified village. It is not hard to imagine Champlain, with his quartermaster's training gained in the army, drawing up plans and directing construction. The site chosen was on a little rise on the north side of the basin, well protected from the north wind by a line of hills. There was an assured supply of water, good soil and a safe anchorage.

Trees were felled, log walls were put up to form an **enclosed rectangle, and buildings were constructed. The** *habitation* at Port Royal was more compact than the one at Ste. Croix had been, and offered more protection from the winds and from attack. The men had learned from experience.

*This is Champlain's picture of the Port Royal habitation. On the basis of Champlain's sketch, the Canadian government built a replica of the settlement in the 1940s. Champlain's lodgings are marked by the letter D.*

In September, the colonists decided that the *habitation* was fit to withstand the winter. De Monts chose to return to France to protect his claims before the king, so Pont-Gravé was made his deputy commander and given charge over the colonists in de Monts' absence. Forty men had come over from France that spring to join the survivors of Ste. Croix. Those who had made it through the previous winter were given the option of returning to France. Only three brave men decided to remain in Canada for a second winter. One of them was Champlain. The others returned thankfully to their homes in Europe.

Champlain spent a busy winter at Port Royal. He had made a large collection of sketch maps and rough notes during his exploration of the New England coast the year before. From these he made good copies, some to aid French navigators, some to include in his report to the king and others to illustrate the book he was already beginning to write. Modern geographers continue to be impressed by the accuracy of the maps that Champlain prepared.

As geographer royal to the expedition, it was Champlain's duty to discover and claim new territories for the king of France. During the winter he spent many hours listening to the Micmacs who visited Port Royal. He paid great attention to any news they could give him of canoe routes to the interior of the continent.

In the spring of 1606, Champlain and Pont-Gravé set out to explore the coast as far south as Florida. They made two attempts. Both ended in failure — one almost in disaster — because of the ineptness of their pilot, Champdoré. Back in Port Royal, Pont-Gravé had the pilot placed in stocks for his misdeeds.

Champlain and the others grew restless during the summer at Port Royal. While most of the men longed to return to France, Champlain itched to get on with his exploring. To console himself and pass the time, he laid out a garden. He writes at length of the pleasure it gave him, revealing a side of his personality not seen in the accounts of exploration and adventure.

Spring passed into summer. The colonists at Port Royal awaited the return of their leader, the Sieur de Monts. The unfortunate pilot, Champdoré, was released from his stocks to build a pinnace, then handcuffed

again when his work was done. June came and went
without any sign of de Monts. In mid-July Champlain
and Port-Gravé decided to return to France, and two
pinnaces were loaded up. Two men volunteered to stay
behind and occupy the fort, maintaining France's claim
to the settlement. They waved good-bye from the shore
as the boats set off on July 17, 1606.

Mountainous seas faced the small craft as they
travelled along the south coast of Nova Scotia. Angry
waters ravaged them, tearing the rudder of the larger
pinnace loose from its irons. Champdoré was released
from his handcuffs to repair the damage, working
bravely under dangerous conditions. Champlain and the
other passengers asked Pont-Gravé to pardon the man

*This sketch shows how solid the
early timber constructions were
The stakes were driven deep into
the ground, as the dotted lines
indicate.*

who made up for his earlier mistakes by saving their
lives on this occasion.

Off the coast of Cape Sable, a sail was sighted. It was a
shallop manned by de Monts' secretary. He told the
crews that Poutrincourt was on his way to Port Royal.
The secretary had been sent to follow the coast in case
the colonists had left already. Together, the three boats
returned to Port Royal to find Poutrincourt's ship, the
*Jonas*, anchored in the harbour.

Poutrincourt had been trying to recruit more settlers
to bring to Port Royal. It had been a difficult task. The
survivors of Ste. Croix had spent many hours in the
seaport taverns of Brittany and Normandy, telling tales
of the harshness of life in the New World. Still,

*The Order of Good Cheer*

Poutrincourt had managed to bring over a group of men eager to face adventure in Canada.

They were a different sort from the men who had passed that first winter at Ste. Croix, on the whole better suited to the task of colonizing. Among them were Poutrincourt's son, Jean, known as Biencourt, and Robert de Pont-Gravé, the son of Champlain's friend. They were joined by Louis Hébert, a druggist from Paris. Hébert would later bring his family to the Quebec settlement and become New France's first farmer. A welcome member of the colony was Marc Lescarbot, a lawyer, poet and scholar, who would later write a book about life at Port Royal. Another recruit was Mathieu d'Acosta, a former Portuguese slave, the first black man to settle in Nova Scotia. He worked as a translator for the colony, having learned the language of the Micmacs while serving on a Portuguese fishing boat. Not all the **crew were so worthy. Some were ruffians who had to be kept in jail in France until the ships were ready to put to sea.**

Poutrincourt soon had all the colonists working hard. Fields were cleared and crops planted. Before long, wheat, rye, cabbages and turnips were sprouting. Lescarbot wrote that the land was fertile and that Poutrincourt had a sensible attitude towards colonizing: wealth could only be obtained from farming, not from the vain search for gold. Champlain's first impressions of the fertility of New France were being confirmed. The rich lands of Canada could support permanent settlements based on farming.

As autumn approached, Poutrincourt divided the colonists into three groups. The first, made up of men who had spent the preceding winter at Port Royal, would return to France. The second group would remain at Port Royal. The third group, led by Poutrincourt, would further explore the coast of North America to the south of Acadia. Champlain chose to face a third winter in the New World and continue his explorations. Only he and two others remained of the group who had gone to Ste. Croix in 1604. One of the other old timers was Champdoré, whom Poutrincourt had chosen to pilot the exploring trip, in spite of his past errors.

Champlain wanted the explorers to head directly to Cape Cod and begin their southward examination of the coast there. He was overruled by Poutrincourt, who elected to retrace the route Champlain had already followed and mapped so carefully. Here Champlain reveals a lack of confidence in his own judgement. He knew the route chosen by Poutrincourt would waste valuable time, but did not press the point. Often, Champlain hesitated to take action, even when he knew he was right.

The voyage began late in the year, in September. It turned out to be worse than just a waste of time. The explorers' encounters with the Indians of Maine were less friendly than those with the Micmacs of Acadia. Dissatisfaction over trade, and the rash actions of some of the crew, led to a battle between the French and the Indians that left three of Poutrincourt's men dead. Others were sick or wounded. To make matters worse, winter was beginning to set in. Early November found them off the coast of Maine with the ice already 5 cm thick. Champlain sadly compared this area with the warmer lands to the south which, if he had had his way, they would have visited and perhaps chosen to colonize.

Snow had already come to Port Royal by mid-November. The colonists who had stayed behind began to worry about their leaders, Poutrincourt and Champlain. Many were ready to give them up for dead. On November 14, a lookout ran back to the *habitation* at Port Royal. "They're safe! They're back! The pinnace has returned," he shouted. Champlain and Poutrincourt made their way into the Annapolis Basin and anchored off Port Royal.

As the weary explorers prepared to go ashore, they stopped in sudden surprise. On the shore the colonists were gathered to welcome them home. A longboat was pushed out from the land, pulling a blue-painted dinghy. Seated in the dinghy was a dramatic figure wearing a long seaweed beard and a blue robe. On his head was a crown; in his hand was a trident.

Neptune, or to be more exact Marc Lescarbot, pulled his boat up alongside Poutrincourt and Champlain as they stepped into their shallop to come ashore. He recited a poem, specially prepared for the occasion, which predicted a great future for France in the New World, under leaders like de Monts, Poutrincourt, and Champlain.

After this dramatic greeting, a cask of wine was opened and a great feast began in honour of the returning explorers. The French colonists were joined by their Micmac allies. To Lescarbot must go the honour of having staged the first play performed in North America; the Neptune Theatre in Halifax commemorates this event.

Champlain, observing the good effects the celebrations had on the morale of the colonists, had an idea. Regular feasts might help to ease the monotony and inactivity of the long Canadian winter. He discussed his idea with Poutrincourt, who was an able musician, and with the poet Lescarbot. Out of these discussions came the Order of Good Cheer.

Every gentleman of the colony became, in turn, Chief Steward and Caterer of the Order of Good Cheer. Wearing the official chain of office, he then had to prepare a menu and provide food for a feast. The stewards competed to provide the best meal. The menus were rich and varied, offering fresh fish, duck, goose, grouse, moose, caribou, venison, beaver tails and the meat of otter, bear, rabbit and wildcat. Most of these dishes were provided by the Micmacs. The Micmac chief, Membertou, and visiting *sagamores* were invited to sit at the head table. Poutrincourt and other musicians played and songs were sung, both old favourites and new ones composed on the spot.

Despite the Order of Good Cheer and an unusually mild winter, scurvy still struck Port Royal. Five men died, including the interpreter d'Acosta.

Spring brought little relief to the colonists. On May 24, 1607, a pinnace from the *Jonas* arrived at Port Royal, bringing bad news. The Sieur de Monts' royal monopoly in the New World had been revoked. Rival fur traders had put pressure on the king to permit competition.

Champlain spent the summer of 1607 making a last search for the copper mines of the Bay of Fundy. He asked that the departure for France be delayed until he could harvest his wheat to show the king just how fertile the soil of Acadia was. Champlain joined the *Jonas* at Canso on the coast of Nova Scotia. Loaded with dried codfish, the ship left Canso on September 3, 1607. Champlain never saw Acadia again.

# On The Warpath Chapter 6

Back in France, Champlain and de Monts persuaded the king to restore the fur monopoly for another year and planned a new expedition to Canada. This time they would concentrate on the St. Lawrence River. Three ships were sent out in the spring of 1608. Two were to trade for furs while the third, commanded by Champlain, was to establish a permanent trading post.

Champlain arrived on July 3, and decided to establish the settlement on a tree-clad promontory which the natives called Quebec. Several large, solid buildings were constructed, some to store provisions and some to serve as living quarters. The settlement was fortified with earth ramparts and moats. As at Ste. Croix, most of the materials were obtained locally, but glazed windows and other fittings were brought from France. While construction was still underway, Champlain put the settlers to work clearing the surrounding land for farms and gardens. He began experimenting with various

*Champlain's drawing of the Quebec habitation*
*The glazed and leaded windows were brought from France, but most of the materials were obtained locally. The settlement was fortified with earth ramparts (M) and cannon positions (N). The letter O denotes Champlain's garden.*

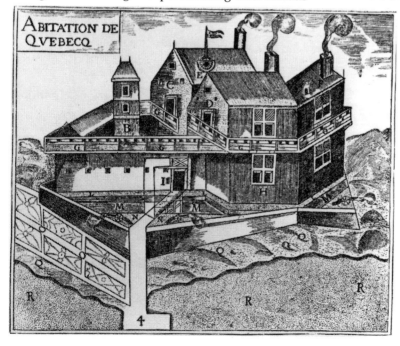

ABITATION DE QVEBECQ

*George A Reid's painting of Champlain's arrival at Quebec*

seeds to find out which plants were best suited to the local climate.

Suddenly, Champlain's leadership was confronted with a serious challenge. Some of his workmen were discontented. They formed a plan to kill Champlain and sell out the colony to the Basques or Spaniards who were then at Tadoussac trading for furs. The leader of the mutiny was Jean Duval, a locksmith. He persuaded four fellow workers to join in his plot.

One of the conspirators, Antoine Natel, could not stand the weight of the guilty secret he carried. He broke down and told Champlain's friend and pilot, Captain Tetsu, of the plan to kill their leader. Tetsu took Champlain aside in the woods near Quebec and told him what Natel had revealed. Champlain summoned Natel, who arrived "all trembling with fear lest I should do him some harm. I reassured him and told him not to be afraid. He was safe and I would forgive him all that he had done with the others . . . provided he told the truth on every point."

Hearing his story, Champlain sent Natel back to his work. Champlain arranged for a trusted sailor to invite the conspirators aboard the pinnace for a party. There were two bottles of wine for them to enjoy, provided by Champlain. At ten that evening, while the plotters were carousing belows decks, Champlain appeared on board the pinnace with a party of armed soldiers. Taken by surprise, the mutineers dared not move. They were bound securely with sailor's knots until the blacksmith could make handcuffs to hold them.

A formal trial was arranged. Champlain asked his friend Pont-Gravé to come from Tadoussac to act as one of the two judges. Champlain was the other. The jury was made up of officers and sailors from the ship, and various witnesses were called from among the workmen who had been approached by the plotters. The men were found guilty. It was decided that Duval should be put to death, as an example to the rest. The other three were also sentenced to hanging, but their sentences were suspended.

This was the first serious test of Champlain's authority. In his handling of it he showed himself to be a man of caution and moderation, anxious to avoid bloodshed.

The *habitation* completed, Champlain and his men settled down to a winter at Quebec. No doubt, as the days grew colder and the nights longer, their thoughts turned to the tragic winter Cartier and his followers had spent on the same spot nearly seventy-five years earlier.

The tragedy was to repeat itself. When spring came, only eight of the twenty-four Frenchmen who spent the winter in the *habitation* at Quebec were left alive. The rest had died of scurvy and dysentery. No-one had avoided the sickness; even Champlain had experienced his first bout of scurvy, after four winters in Canada.

Champlain spent the winter learning and recording the ways of the native peoples of New France. Long hours were spent asking questions of the friendly Montagnais who gathered around the *habitation*. Two young French settlers of fifteen or so shared these lessons. They were Etienne Brûlé and Nicolas Marsolet, both of whom would become important explorers of Canada. During the long winter, the two learned the Montagnais language, something Champlain was never able to do, and became valued interpreters.

From his discussions, Champlain learned more of the traditional wars between the Algonquin and the Iroquois. He concluded that helping the Algonquin, and their allies the Huron, defeat the Iroquois was essential for the success of the French fur trading venture.

In the spring of 1609, a party of Huron leaders came to call on Champlain at Batiscan, 120 km upstream from Quebec. Champlain realized the importance of this visit. There were solemn greetings. Presents were exchanged, and Champlain smoked the peace pipe in silent ritual with his visitors. The leaders told Champlain that they had heard of his promises to help the Algonquin and Huron people defeat their enemies, the Iroquois. The Huron chief, Ochateguin, and the Algonquin chief, Iroquet, proposed that the group should return to the *habitation* at Quebec. From there, the Huron, the Algonquin and the French would go on the warpath against the Iroquois. Champlain agreed.

At Quebec, four or five days of feasting elapsed before the expedition began. Champlain grew impatient, so eager was he to be back in action after the long winter. At length, the war party set out for the land of the Iroquois. The two groups presented a striking contrast:

*Champlain's picture of the battle against the Iroquois at Lake Champlain*

*The figure in the centre firing the gun is Champlain: this is the only self-portrait known to exist. The other two French arquebusiers are concealed in the trees. The feather headdresses of the two fallen figures in front of Champlain indicate that they are chiefs. Behind the Iroquois is their wooden enclosure. Note the streamlined birch canoes of the Huron (H) in comparison with the snub-nosed, clumsier elm canoes of the Iroquois (C).*

the Indians in their agile birch-bark canoes; the French in their steel corselets and helmets, carrying clumsy arquebuses, powder, lead shot and heavy baggage in the awkward shallop. At Chambly Rapids on the Richelieu the shallop could go no farther. Champlain called for volunteers to go with him and the sixty-odd Huron, Algonquin, and Ottawa Indians in combat against the Iroquois. Of the twelve who accompanied him, only three volunteered. The rest shook in fear at the thought of the adventure; in Champlain's words, "their noses bled." He sent them back to Quebec in the shallop.

Champlain and his companions pressed on with their Indian allies. Paddling up the broad Richelieu, they soon entered a lake. For two weeks, they travelled south along the lakeshore. Champlain was impressed by the lake's size and beauty. In his journal, he comments on its beautiful islands and rivers. Looking east, he could see the hills of Vermont and the Adirondacks. Moved by its beauty, Champlain gave the lake his own name: Lake Champlain it remains to this day. The Indians with Champlain pointed to the Adirondacks. There, they said, Champlain would meet the Iroquois. Now the war party was in hostile territory. It travelled by night, out of sight of watching Iroquois eyes. Daytime was spent hidden safely, deep in the forest.

Just after sunset on July 29, the invaders were paddling silently southward near Ticonderoga. Out of the deepening darkness to the south came shouts and war cries. They had been sighted by a war party of Mohawk Iroquois. The Iroquois, whose clumsy elm-bark canoes were no match on the water for the swift birch canoes of the Huron, pulled ashore. They built a barricade, cutting down trees with their stone axes. Champlain and his Huron companions waited off shore. Soon two Iroquois canoes were sent out to negotiate. Finding the Huron eager for battle, they agreed to begin fighting at daybreak. Champlain slept little. All night long, the Iroquois danced and sang on the shore. His allies replied with insulting songs.

At dawn, the Huron and their allies went ashore, unhindered by the Iroquois. They formed their battle lines. Gravely, the Iroquois marched out from behind their barricade. There were two hundred of them, outnumbering Champlain's allies by three to one. Champlain, hidden in the woods, looked on:

They came slowly to meet us with a gravity and calm which I admired. At their head were three chiefs. Our Indians likewise advanced in similar order. They had told me that . . . I was to try to kill the chiefs if I could. I promised to do all in my power and told them I was sorry they could not understand me, as I would like to be able to direct the attack. I was sure that we could kill all of them, but there was no way to overcome this problem. I was very glad to show them, as soon as the battle began, the courage and readiness that were in me.

When the battle commenced, Champlain's two French companions remained in the woods with some of the Indians. Champlain marched forward with the rest, who kept him hidden until the last moment. The sudden sight of this strange man dressed in shiny metal clothing startled the Iroquois. As he approached, all of their attention was turned towards him. Iroquois bows were raised and arrows readied. Without warning, Champlain fired his arquebus in the direction of one of the chiefs. He had loaded his weapon with four bullets. With one burst, two of the chiefs were killed immediately and a third fell to the ground wounded, to die later. As Champlain paused to reload, one of the Frenchmen in the woods fired his arquebus at the Iroquois. Terrified by this strange new weapon against which their shields could not protect them, the Iroquois fled into the depths of the forest. Champlain pursued them, killing several more before they escaped.

The Huron celebrated the event as a great victory,

*Reconstruction on the original site of Champlain's habitation at Port Royal.*

feasting on corn meal that the Iroquois had abandoned in their flight. They danced and sang for three hours before heading north for home. On the way home Champlain, who had earlier taken joy in the sudden death he had brought to the Iroquois, watched in disgust as the Huron tortured a prisoner. His allies invited him to take burning sticks from the fire and join them in the torture. He urged them to let him kill the prisoner and put him out of his misery. The Huron refused, saying that death would spare their prisoner his pain. Champlain stormed away from the scene in anger, but returned when the Huron relented. He killed the man with a single shot from his arquebus, then looked on in horror as the man's body was cut up. His brother and several other prisoners were forced to eat pieces of the man's heart.

Champlain spent the winter of 1609 in France, where he learned that de Monts' monopoly was not to be renewed. Free trade had come to the St. Lawrence once again. When he returned to Quebec in 1610, he found that his success in the battle with the Iroquois had made him famous. He was known as the "man who kept his word." The Montagnais and Algonquin praised him highly, reminding him at the same time of his promise to go with them on the warpath against their enemies, bringing with him, of course, the marvellous stick that created thunder and brought death to the Iroquois.

Champlain would have preferred to resume his search for the salt sea which he had first heard about seven years earlier, but the native people were wary about letting Europeans travel too far into their territory. The European intruders were tolerated only as military allies and trading partners. Had Champlain been allowed to satisfy his curiosity, he might have beaten the English to Hudson Bay. Instead, he agreed to go on the warpath. The Algonquin and Huron were so eager to attack the Iroquois that they rushed on ahead. Champlain and the other French arquebusiers were weighed down by their heavy armour and weapons. Plagued by insects and delayed by swampy ground, they fell far behind the Indians. The Huron and Algonquin attacked a hastily constructed Iroquois fortress of logs and brush without waiting for the arquebuses. The Iroquois easily beat off the attack.

As they approached the fortress, Champlain and his party could hear great howls and shouts. The Huron had retreated and were trading insults with their enemy while waiting for their allies to arrive. Champlain wrote at length of the ensuing battle in his report to the king:

As I was firing my first shot near the barricade, I was wounded by an arrow that split the tip of my ear and entered my neck. I seized the arrow, which was still stuck in my neck, and pulled it out. At the same time, one of my companions took an arrow in the arm and I pulled it out for him also. My wound did not hinder me, however, from doing my duty. Our Indian allies also did theirs, and the Iroquois, too, fought well. The battle was so fierce that we could see the arrows on all sides flying as thick as hailstones. The Iroquois were greatly startled by the sounds of our arquebuses. But they were more astonished because our bullets penetrated better than their arrows. They were so frightened at the killing done by our bullets, seeing several of their companions fall dead or wounded, that they would throw themselves to the ground at the sound of a shot. Besides, we hardly missed a shot firing two or three bullets each time.

Champlain and his men stood at the barricade resting the barrels of the arquebuses on the logs. Under the cover of the arquebus fire, the Huron soon breached the barricade. A cease-fire was ordered, and the attackers entered the fort with drawn swords. The Iroquois tried to escape but were trapped by their own defensive barrier. Many who did escape were drowned in the river. Of an estimated one hundred Iroquois, only fifteen were alive to be taken prisoner.

All the traditions of Indian warfare had been shattered by Champlain's arquebuses. Even the log fortifications which had once offered safety could now be taken. Mass slaughter, long a part of European warfare, had come to North America. Traditional warfare involving primitive weapons had inflicted relatively few injuries or deaths. The purpose of war had been to humiliate the enemy; the winner took a few captives and fled home to celebrate the victory. All this had now changed. Battles could be fought until one side was wiped out. The Iroquois vowed revenge. Their anger would keep the French from effectively penetrating the St. Lawrence past the Lachine Rapids.

# Chapter 7 **Hélène**

Champlain returned to France in the fall of 1610 to find things greatly changed. His old friend and protector, King Henri, had been assassinated. The new king was a young boy. Rumours in the taverns of Honfleur whispered that Henri's assassin was in the pay of the Jesuits, and that the new king's mother was plotting to steal France's war reserves. Everyone was talking about plots and counterplots and wondering who was actually running the country.

Things looked bad for de Monts, Champlain's employer and patron. King Henri had been a friend, a strong supporter of de Monts' and Champlain's efforts to colonize North America for France. Adding to de Monts' dismay was the fact that the cost of fur trading had gone up greatly. Free trade had meant increased competition. The price of a prime beaver pelt had increased from one or two knives to fifteen or twenty. And an increased supply of furs to France led to lower prices in Paris. Still, the last year's trade had been profitable, and Champlain's good relations with the Huron and Algonquin gave de Monts a definite advantage. Reluctantly, de Monts and his partners agreed to carry on for another year. Champlain would return to Quebec in the spring as usual.

Before he did so, however, Samuel de Champlain had an important bit of business to take care of. Now approaching his mid-forties, the bachelor explorer decided it was time to marry. His search and negotiations led him to the home of a Parisian secretary to the royal court, Nicolas Boullé. It was agreed that Champlain should marry the well-to-do bourgeois family's daughter, Hélène. She was twelve years old.

A marriage contract was drawn up and signed on December 27, 1610. Hélène's father was to provide a dowry of 6000 livres. The two were not to live together until Champlain's child bride reached the age of fourteen. It snowed heavily the day the contract was signed, reminding Champlain of his beloved Quebec. He must have told Hélène of the even greater snows she would one day experience in New France. Three days later, Champlain and Hélène Boullé were married in St. Germain-l'Auxerrois, the parish church of the kings of France.

That winter Champlain and his young wife explored Paris. They shared the pageantry of the royal court and of the cathedral, Notre Dame, and strolled through the courtyard of the Louvre, where a carousel had been set up for the boy-king Louis. They were joined on their outings by a companion from the New World, Savignon, the son of Chief Iroquet. Champlain and Savignon taught Hélène about life in New France while the young Indian learned the French language and customs.

Savignon did not much like what he saw in France. Both he and Champlain were eager to return to Quebec the following spring. Late in February, Champlain said good-bye to Hélène, for he felt that the facilities in Quebec were not yet ready to receive her. She would have to wait until 1620 to see the land her husband loved so much.

The crossing in March of 1611 was a very rough one. Champlain sailed early, hoping to beat the other traders to the St. Lawrence. As a result, his ship encountered heavy ice off the coast of Canada and giant icebergs daily threatened to crush it. The decks and rigging were encrusted with ice, making the ship difficult to handle. The ice floes were so thick that "more than a score of times we thought we would not come out alive."

Champlain was committed to four goals in New France. The first he owed to his sponsors. He was to expand and protect the profitable fur trade. To do so, he was to enter into alliances with the Indians of the area and if necessary offer military aid to ensure their support. Second, for himself and his king, he was committed to exploring and mapping the new lands of North America. His great desire was to find a route to China and the riches of the Pacific. Third, he had a personal dream, a goal that had stayed with him since his first visit to the St. Lawrence in 1603: he hoped to establish permanent farming settlements on the rich lands of the St. Lawrence River valley. Fourth, Champlain, perhaps himself a convert to Catholicism, hoped to see the day when the Indians of New France would all embrace the Christian religion.

The first spring back in Canada after his marriage, Champlain concentrated on the fur trade. From Quebec he pushed west to the Lachine Rapids. There, on the site of what is now Montreal, he decided to establish an annual fur-trading fair. When the Indians gathered for the first trade fair, he promised to build a second *habitation* at Montreal. The promise was well received since a permanent settlement would deter the Iroquois from attacking Huron bringing furs to trade. As it turned out, the *habitation* at Montreal would not be built in Champlain's lifetime. He named an island in the river near Montreal Ile Sainte-Hélène after his bride.

Moving further upstream, Champlain met with his Indian allies to plan future strategies against the Iroquois. His real interest, however, was in finding out what lay beyond the river to the west. Through his interpreter, Etienne Brûlé, Champlain learned about the geography of the area around the Great Lakes. He left Brûlé behind with the Indians to learn more of the region and of the people who inhabited it.

On his return trip to Montreal, the Indians offered to

*This pen-and-ink sketch by C.W. Jefferys shows Champlain taking an observation with his astrolabe, an instrument which navigators and surveyors used to find their location from the stars.*

show Champlain a short cut. It involved running the treacherous Lachine Rapids in birch-bark canoes. Champlain tried as politely as possible to suggest he was in no hurry, for the great sailor had never learned to swim, but the Indians were eager to test the courage of their ally. Champlain realized that refusal to go through the rapids would be taken as a sign of cowardice, so he agreed to go with them. The Indians stripped naked; Champlain took off his boots and armour but modestly left on his shirt. The party set off through the rapids in eight birch-bark canoes. Champlain hung on for dear life as the canoe left quiet water and passed between walls of rock where the water foamed high. He kept reminding himself of the advice the Indians had given him: hang on to the canoe if it goes over, and we will save you. He watched as the canoe seemed to shoot over the horizon, then felt it drop safely to quieter waters below. Having risked his life to avoid losing face with the Indians, he had come through unharmed. He was the first European to run the Lachine Rapids and survive.

The fur-trading season over, Champlain returned to France in the fall of 1611. Arriving at La Rochelle, he went first to Pons to report to de Monts, then set out for home. Riding along the great western highway, Champlain's horse stumbled and fell, rolling on top of him. Champlain was seriously injured and lay on the roadside near death. He was found by a passerby and taken to a roadside inn, where he lay ill, only a short distance from Paris, throughout the fall and winter. What an ironic twist of fate: he had survived crushing icebergs and the perils of the Lachine Rapids, only to be nearly killed by his own horse close to home.

Champlain was reunited with his thirteen-year-old wife in Paris in the spring of 1612. He brought her gifts: beaded moccasins, a sweetgrass basket decorated with porcupine quills. Together, Hélène and Champlain attended a three-day festival in the Place Royale celebrating the engagement of the young king of France to a Spanish princess. There were mock battles between knights on horseback, music, dancing and theatrical performances. On stage, a mechanical volcano spouted fire and water. A ballet was performed, with dancers dressed as Indians from New France. Champlain pointed out to Hélène the errors in their costume.

There was work as well as play for Champlain. He was trying to win support for the construction of a fur-trading fort at Montreal, and for his plan to raise an army to defeat the Iroquois. The king made Champlain *lieutenant du roi* in New France, with all the powers of a ruler. He could make laws, set up a system of justice, wage wars and negotiate treaties. He was authorized to search for a route to China and the Indies, and to seek gold and other precious minerals.

Champlain returned to Quebec in the spring of 1613. Despite his royal commission, and all the powers it carried with it on paper, he did not have the manpower or money to build a fort at Montreal. Nor did he have enough soldiers to fight the Iroquois. He found himself in a tight spot, unable to keep his promises to his Indian allies.

During his absence, rival fur traders had told the Indians that Champlain was dead, hoping to get their trade. The Indians were surprised and overjoyed to see their friend return. Now, at last, the Iroquois would be defeated.

Champlain, knowing that he could not fight the Iroquois, had other plans. He decided to set out on an exploratory trip into Huronia in the hope of reassuring and encouraging his Indian trading partners. With two canoes, four French paddlers and an Indian guide, Champlain set off westward. The canoes were heavily loaded, packed with food, weapons, and gifts for the Indian chiefs he might meet. He hoped to travel north as far as Hudson Bay, mapping the route as he went. One of his paddlers, Nicolas Vigneau, claimed to have travelled to the northern sea the year before.

Heading further and further north, Champlain began to doubt Vigneau's story. The young man claimed that the sea was only eight days journey north of Montreal. They had already been travelling for ten days, and there was no sign of the sea. Upstream, they encountered severe rapids and were forced to portage for 10 km, laden with provisions and equipment. The men had to struggle through thick brush in burning heat, tormented by mosquitoes.

Champlain and his crew returned to the Ottawa River near the modern town of Perreton. There he met an old friend, Tessouat, the one-eyed king of the

*This is the very astrolabe that
Champlain took with him on his
expedition north in 1613.
During a particularly difficult
portage, Champlain dropped the
instrument. It lay undisturbed
for 253 years, until 1866, when
it was found by a sharp-eyed
fourteen-year-old farmboy.*

Allumette Algonquin. Champlain and Tessouat had met
ten years earlier at Tadoussac, on Champlain's first visit
to New France. Tessouat and his people told him that
Vigneau was lying and tried to discourage Champlain
from heading north himself. When confronted, Vigneau
admitted his deceit. Champlain was bitterly
disappointed. Tessouat, on the other hand, was pleased.
The last thing he wanted was the French taking over his
very profitable fur-trading territory.

Frustrated once more in his efforts to explore the
territory surrounding his colony, Champlain headed
back down the Ottawa River. He returned safely to the
St. Lawrence in time to supervise a profitable trading
season.

On the way back to France at the end of the season,
Champlain worked hard on his journal. That fall his
second book, *Voyages du Sieur de Champlain*, was
published. Drawn from his journals, it tells of
Champlain's experiences in Canada between 1603 and
1613. It contains many maps and drawings, including
illustrations of the settlements at Ste. Croix, Port Royal
and Quebec. The book sold well and many copies have
survived to the present day.

# Chapter 8 The Inland Sea

Champlain remained in France through 1614, returning to Quebec the following year. He had arranged for a group of friars, the Recollets, to travel to New France. As missionaries, they would attempt to convert the Indians to Christianity.

The colony leader's concerns were, for the time being, less spiritual. The Huron were pleased to see Champlain return, but at the fur fair, at Montreal, they demanded that he make good his promise to go on the warpath with them. The Indians intended to raise an army of 2500 warriors. Before he returned to Quebec, Champlain assured them he would bring as many French soldiers as he could. Over the next two weeks he made arrangements for the running of the colony in his absence. He found only two men willing to go with him to war, Etienne Brûlé and Thomas Godefroy. Ten of the Indians camped at Quebec agreed to accompany them.

Meanwhile, the Huron at Montreal had left the Lachine Rapids for their homes. They were upset at Champlain's delay in returning, fearing he had been killed or captured by the Iroquois. Accompanied by one of the priests, Father Joseph le Caron, and twelve French soldiers, they set off for the Great Lakes with one week's head start on Champlain.

The route that Champlain had to follow was a roundabout one. The Iroquois controlled the upper St. Lawrence River, blocking that path to the lakes, so that Champlain was forced to go north and then west. He followed the Ottawa River, which became progressively narrower and more boulder-strewn. They were now passing through the bleak landscape of the Canadian Shield. "It was," says Champlain in his journal, "a very disagreeable region." At Mattawa they left the Ottawa River and continued westward along the Mattawa River. On July 26, 1615, seventeen days after leaving Montreal, Champlain had his first view of the great freshwater sea at the heart of North America. He had come to the place where the city of North Bay, Ontario, would one day be built. He reached the shores of Lake Huron two days later.

He was not the first European to see the Great Lakes. Brûlé had been there four years earlier, and Father le Caron and his twelve French soldiers had been there a week before Champlain. Nevertheless, it was an important occasion. Champlain had dreamed of reaching the "inland sea" for twelve years, ever since his first visit to Canada.

Champlain met up with Father le Caron at the village of Carhagouha, in Huronia, which had already been fortified against Iroquois attack. The Indians had built a bark-covered longhouse for use as a chapel. Champlain attended the first Catholic mass in what is now Ontario on August 12.

Champlain and the Huron chiefs held a war council in the chief village of Huronia, Cahiague. The Huron, Champlain soon found out, were not really ready to go

*Champlain's drawing of the 1615 assault on a fortified Iroquois village in the modern state of New York*

*As soon as he saw the Iroquois's strongly walled fortress, Champlain realized that even his guns would be unable to break it down. Remembering the campaigns he had fought in Brittany, he instructed his Indian allies to build a portable tower, called a cavalier, from pieces of wood bound together with vines. From the top of the cavalier (shown in the picture at bottom right), the French arquebusiers could fire over the top of the palisade, forcing the Iroquois to flee for shelter.*

to war. The single week's delay in his arrival had again led them to believe that he was dead or a prisoner of the Iroquois, and had dampened their enthusiasm for battle.

He realized that he had to rally his Huron allies to the attack. Defeat of the Iroquois was necessary to French plans for controlling the fur trade, for the French depended on the furs the Huron supplied. We can only wonder if the Huron's unreadiness resulted from a growing suspicion that the French were more interested in the furs than in the Indians. Champlain made a speech to the Huron chiefs, telling them, "It is not too late. With my fourteen men and their fourteen guns we can attack the enemy stronghold. We can bring terror to their country, as they have to ours."

After consideration, the chiefs agreed that the time was right for the attack. They told Champlain that they had allies, the Carantouans, living to the south who had promised to send five hundred warriors to help them fight the Iroquois. Champlain urged the Huron to contact their allies immediately. Now, when he was impatient to go on the warpath, the Huron were in no hurry. "First we must feast, and sing, and dance," they said. And feast and sing and dance they did, for a week, while Champlain sat fuming at the delay. When the last drum beat stopped and the warriors made ready to leave, Champlain had further cause for anger. Instead of the promised 2500 warriors, only 500 were ready to go to war.

The party headed south, towards Iroquois country. Brûlé was sent off to meet with the Carantouans and bring them to the battle field. The expedition into Iroquois territory gave Champlain time to view but not explore many new parts of the country. The war party travelled through the Bay of Quinte, then crossed Lake Ontario through the Thousand Islands. Entering upstate New York, they surprised a group of Iroquois fishing on Oneida Lake and took eleven prisoners. Near the present city of Syracuse, New York, they spotted a fortified Iroquois village. Here, the war party stopped to plan an attack.

Champlain's suggestion was simple. The Huron and the French soldiers would hide in the woods during the night. At dawn, they would launch a surprise attack on the target.

The assault did not go according to plan. As the attackers neared the fort they were ambushed by a party of Iroquois braves, and the element of surprise was lost. The Iroquois fortification proved much stronger than Champlain had expected. Its outer barricade was made of two leaning walls of tree trunks which crossed 5 m above the ground. The space between the walls was filled with logs. The Iroquois had learned all about arquebuses, both from their clashes with Champlain and from their Dutch allies. This fortress was strong enough to protect them against gunshots. Sensing that their leaders' plan was not working, the Huron warriors began to panic. Many were wounded in the storm of arrows the Iroquois fired off from behind the walls. Champlain himself was wounded twice in the leg.

The attackers retreated to await reinforcements. They never came. Champlain was forced to concede defeat. Amid hail, cold rain and snow flurries, Champlain and his Huron allies retreated across Lake Ontario. Champlain's wounds forced him to be carried back to the canoes in a sort of chair strapped to the back of an Indian warrior. He wrote afterwards of a sense of humiliation almost as great as the pain from his injuries.

Four years would pass before Champlain would see Brûlé again, and find out why the promised support never came. It turned out that the Carantouans had spent so much time feasting and singing and dancing

*Martyrdom of the Jesuit Missionaries, by Grégoire Huret. Many of the missionaries who attempted to convert the Indians to Christianity came to unpleasant ends, as this engraving illustrates. The gruesome picture is a reminder of the very real dangers which faced the early explorers and colonists.*

before setting off on the warpath that they reached the
battlefield two days after Champlain had left in defeat.

The loss created a rift of bad feelings between the
French and the Huron. The Indians felt betrayed. They
had been confidently promised victory, and now they
were forced to retreat, looking foolish. Some of the
Huron even suggested that Champlain was secretly in
league with the Iroquois. When Champlain asked to be
taken back to Quebec, the Huron refused. Instead they
took him west, into Huronia, where he was to spend the

*Champlain's great 1613 map of
New France.*

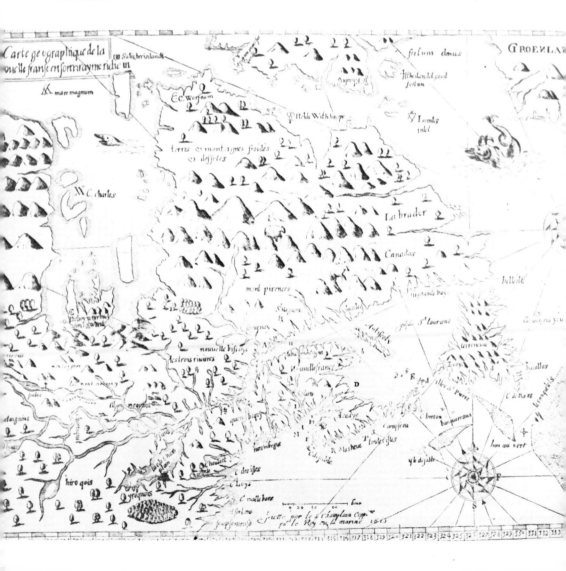

winter of 1615-16. He realized that his own prestige and that of all the French colonists had suffered because of the defeat, and he felt the humiliation deeply.

Champlain passed the winter months restlessly in the longhouse of chief Darontal in Cahiague. To occupy themselves, he and Father Caron decided to accompany a tribe of Nipissing Indians on their annual trading trip to Hudson Bay. Just as they were setting out, however, in January of 1616, bad news came from Cahiague. The Huron and Algonquin, both French allies, were at each others' throats. If war broke out, the French fur trade was in danger of being destroyed. Champlain rushed back to Cahiague. He found that the trouble had started over an Iroquois warrior, captured by the Huron. The prisoner had been presented to the Algonquin in the expectation that he would be tortured and eaten in the approved manner. But Iroquet, the Algonquin chief, had taken a liking to the captive. He spared his life and had even allowed him to hunt with his tribe. The Huron sent a man to kill the Iroquois prisoner in front of Iroquet, in response to this breach of etiquette. In turn, the Huron killer was murdered by the Iroquois prisoner as he died.

Champlain called together the leaders of the Huron and Algonquin. He made a long speech in which he pointed out that because of the death of two men, many thousands could be killed if war broke out. He argued that honour had been upheld, since both men were dead. Further, he noted, the Algonquin had eaten the Iroquois prisoner's body, keeping the tradition intact. He begged both parties to forget all that had happened and remain good friends.

Champlain's solution was applauded by both sides. Peace was restored, along with Champlain's good name among his Indian allies, and the French fur trade with the Huron was preserved. Champlain remained for the rest of the winter as an honoured guest in Darontal's lodge in Cahiague. There he made sketches and recorded his observations of Huron life.

Spring came, the ice left the rivers, and Champlain and his French companions set off on a leisurely trip back to Quebec, reaching Montreal at the end of June. Champlain was welcomed back by his old friend Pont-Gravé, who was overjoyed at Champlain's safe return. On his return to Quebec, he was delighted to find that

*The top sketch of an Iroquois village shows the construction of the double wall in detail. The platform running round the inside of the palisade allowed defenders to fire arrows down on attackers. The bottom picture shows a reconstructed Huron village at Midland, Ontario.*

the first woman settler, Marguerite Vienne, had arrived at the colony. Unfortunately, she fell ill and died just before the ship carrying Champlain home left for France.

He spent the winter of 1616-17 in France, where he recruited an old friend, Louis Hébert, as a settler for the New France colony. Hébert, who had been with Champlain at Port Royal, sailed for Quebec in the spring of 1617 with his wife, two daughters and a young son. Champlain stayed behind to lobby more support for the colony.

He returned to New France for the fur fair of 1618, crossing the Atlantic with Pont-Gravé. When he landed, Champlain found the *habitation* in a neglected condition and immediately gave orders for repairs and improvements to be made. Not for the first time, Champlain felt that he was maintaining the colony singlehanded. His disappointment was eased by the achievements of the Héberts. They had cleared land and begun farming, and one of the daughters had married a colonist. At last, his dream of a permanent French settlement in Canada seemed to be coming true.

Returning to France in the fall, Champlain spent the winter working on his third book, *Voyages and Discoveries made in New France, from 1615 to 1618*. It was a handsome book, filled with illustrations showing the life of the native peoples of Canada. It was dedicated to the king himself, in an effort to win more support for the colony. The response was a strengthening of Champlain's position in New France. He was appointed governor of Quebec, with control over everything but the merchants' warehouse. As most of the men at Quebec worked for the merchants, Champlain's real powers were limited. Once again, failure to provide funds and soldiers meant that the colony remained weak in the face of growing English and Iroquois strength.

# Quebec Changes Hands

## Chapter 9

By 1620, Champlain felt that the colony was fit to receive the most important settler of all, his wife Hélène. She was now twenty-two years old and had been Champlain's wife for ten years, but she had spent only a few winters with her husband. Now she was to accompany him to Quebec and preside over the governor's house in proper style. Accompanied by three ladies-in-waiting and a maid, Hélène Champlain and her husband set sail for Canada.

Her first view of the colony brought tears to her eyes. They were not tears of joy. On the Atlantic crossing, Champlain had pictured the *habitation* to her as a kind of chateau in the wilderness. She arrived to find it abandoned and in disrepair. The settlers had built small stone houses on their farms, and the priests were living in their own convent. The *habitation*, the only building large enough for the governor's quarters, was empty. Rain poured in through cracks in the boards. It looked, in Champlain's own words, "like some poor house abandoned in the fields after being used by soldiers."

Champlain set the labourers to work repairing it. The Champlains had brought beds, linens, drapes and furniture from France to grace their house, but not even the finest silks could hide the rough edges of life in the colony from Hélène's eyes.

Hélène de Champlain spent four miserable years in the Quebec colony. Accustomed to the society of seventeenth-century France, she missed having someone of her own station to talk to. Madame Hébert and the other women of the colony were considered to be beneath her, although she did agree to stand godmother to a child born to the Desportes family in 1620. If she did not feel at home with her own people, however, she was gracious to the Indians. One of her favorite pieces of jewellery was a small mirror that hung from a necklace. The Indians loved to look into it, seeing their own faces reflected. An Indian woman asked Hélène why she could see her own face there. She replied, "Because you are always near my heart."

While Hélène suffered greatly in the limited company and snowbound monotony of the *habitation*, Champlain was content to rule over his house and his tiny colony. He kept a careful diary of the coming of spring in 1624, revealing again his sensitivity to nature.

Hélène's discontent grew deeper. She was homesick, longing daily for Parisian society, for her friends and family. Champlain decided to return to France in the spring of 1624, taking a thankful Hélène with him.

The Champlains established themselves in a comfortable and elegant house in Paris on the Rue de la Marche. Once again, Champlain spent the winter seeking support for the colony; this time he also spent time with Hélène, trying to make up for the misery the stay at Quebec had caused her. The differences between them proved too great. After a while, Hélène offered to enter a convent. Divorce was not possible in Catholic France at that time; the nearest thing was for one or the other spouse to enter religious life, thus effectively ending the marriage.

Champlain returned alone to the colony in 1626. Pont-Gravé, now almost eighty and crippled with gout, hobbled out to meet him on his return. Champlain found that the *habitation* had again fallen into disrepair during his absence.

In 1627, Champlain was saddened by the death of his old companion, Louis Hébert. Canada's first French farmer, Hébert had played an important part in the creation of a permanent settlement at Quebec. His daughters had married colonists; their children and grandchildren would be born and grow up in Quebec. After Hébert's death his widow stayed in the colony, for Canada had become her home.

The winter of 1628 was a severe one. Many of the native people suffered from starvation. Champlain provided them with some food from the colony's scant supplies and in return they gave him three young Indian girls. Champlain treated the girls as the children he and Hélène had never had. They, in turn, looked upon him as their father. He named them Faith, Hope and Charity and instructed them in the Christian faith. He also tried to give them the education that young French women would have received. An amusing and touching sight in the *habitation* that winter was Champlain tracing designs for his "daughters" to embroider in wool.

In the spring of 1628, the colonists anxiously waited for the first supply ship to arrive from France. Provisions were quickly running out; if the ship did not come soon, the colony would have to be abandoned. Champlain ordered the construction of a boat that could take the settlers to Gaspé should the need arise. There, they would be able to find French fishermen to carry them home.

At last, two cowherds from Cap Tourmente approached Champlain. With them came an Indian who had paddled all the way from Tadoussac to bring the news. "The ships have arrived," he said, "Six ships, under the command of Michel de Dieppe."

The settlers at Quebec were greatly relieved, but after his initial excitement Champlain began to have misgivings. "Something's wrong here," he wrote, "Why six ships, when ordinarily there are only two or three? And why Michel de Dieppe as commander?" He was not the sort of person for so important a charge.

His suspicions aroused, Champlain ordered his interpreter to disguise himself as an Indian and make his way to Tadoussac in a canoe. He was to investigate the arrival of the six ships. Meanwhile, Champlain put the fort in order at Quebec. All the men were placed on full alert; the women were taken to safety.

Soon the interpreter returned. Wounded in his canoe lay Foucher, the commander at Cap Tourmente. His post had been attacked by the English. The invaders had been accompanied by Frenchmen. Traitors!

Foucher and his men had found themselves surrounded by armed invaders. They were threatened and forced to surrender. The English killed some of the cattle on the spot, then drove the rest of the frightened animals into barns where they were burned alive. The houses at the cape were burned and everything in them destroyed. The settlers were dragged aboard the attackers' ships. In the confusion, Foucher, though he was injured, managed to escape.

Hearing this story, Champlain sounded the alarm. His men set to work strengthening the defences. Trenches were deepened and barricades reinforced.

*This likeness, by the eighteenth-century portrait painter Louis César Ducornet, and entitled, by him, "Samuel de Champlain, Gouverneur Général du Canada," has formed the basis for all other Champlain pictures, and is the portrait usually used to represent the explorer.*

*But Ducornet — who obviously could not have seen Champlain in the flesh — claimed to have copied his portrait from a picture of Champlain painted by an artist called Moncornet. No such painting — nor any record of it — has ever been found; but another portrait by Moncornet (of Michel Particelli) has been shown to bear a strong likeness to Ducornet's portrait of Champlain.*

*Modern scholars have suggested that Ducornet in fact used the Particelli portrait as his model, and conclude that no true portrait of Samuel de Champlain exists.*

Anxiously, he checked his supply of ammunition. He had just over 20 kg of gunpowder and precious little equipment.

On July 10, 1628, the day after Foucher's escape, a small boat approached Quebec. Champlain hailed the oarsmen and asked them to come ashore. When they landed they explained to him that they were Basques whose ship had been captured by the English. They had been ordered to bring a letter to the French leader from the English captain, David Kirke.

Champlain read the letter aloud to the men assembled at Quebec. It announced that the writer had received a licence from the king of England to take possession of Canada and Acadia. The letter told Champlain that the English had killed the cattle at Cap Tourmente because, "I know when you are short of food, I shall more easily get what I want — which is, to take your settlement." Kirke's letter continued:

I am determined to stay here until the navigation season has ended, so no ship may bring you food. Wherefore, consider now what you wish to do, whether or not you are willing to surrender Quebec. For sooner or later, with God's help, I must have it. I hope for your sake that it shall fall to good grace and not to force, so as to avoid bloodshed on both sides. If you surrender the place with courtesy, you may rest assured of receiving good treatment of yourself and of your goods. On my faith, and on my hope of paradise, I shall keep them as surely as if they were my own, without losing the smallest piece. Awaiting your reply, and your decision to do the above stated, I shall remain, Sirs, your affectionate servant. . . .

With calculated politeness, Kirke was letting Champlain know that he would use the oldest and easiest means of bringing an opponent to his knees: blockade and starvation.

Champlain's response was as courteous as Kirke's letter. Reduced to simple terms, his elegant reply said the French would not surrender, but would stand and fight. Quebec was a superb natural fortress, well protected against attack.

Kirke and his crew were impressed by Champlain's boldness. They had come in search of furs and loot. The last thing they wanted was to die on the barricades of Quebec. Deciding to leave the settlement to starve itself into submission, Kirke set out from Tadoussac to capture any French ships that might enter the Gulf of St. Lawrence.

Meanwhile, Cardinal Richelieu had sent four ships

with 200 settlers and supplies to reinforce and supply the colony at Quebec. A new company, the Company of One Hundred Associates, had been formed to run the colony and the fur trade. The company was given control over the fur trade forever, and over all other resources of Canada, except fish, for fifteen years. In return, they were to send out 200 settlers a year. At the end of fifteen years there were to be 4000 settlers living in the colony. Three priests were to be supported in each settlement, and any Indians they converted were to have all the rights of French citizens. The first group of settlers sent over by the Company of One Hundred Associates was entering the gulf as Kirke and his ships set out from Tadoussac.

Kirke met the fleet off the coast of Gaspé. The battle lasted fourteen hours, and when it was over the French were beaten. All of the ships but one were captured.

As fall wore on, Champlain became increasingly aware that help from France could no longer be expected. He anxiously reviewed the situation. There were seventy-five French men, women and children in the settlement, along with two Indian girls and an Indian prisoner accused of murdering two settlers. To feed them through the winter, he had only a few barrels of dried peas in the storehouse. He was able to buy 1200 dried eels from the Montagnais, paying with beaver pelts, and a farm near the fort had a little surplus food. The total supply worked out to 250 g of food a week for the whole company. In his journal Champlain notes, "This was a very small amount among so many people."

All other food had to come from the land and the river. The settlers fished and hunted, but there was little game to be shot and ammunition was too precious to waste. As the settlers grew hungry, men traded their coats to the Indians for food. The Indians taught the settlers how to find edible roots in the woods. The fare was sparse and, from the sounds of menus like "peas, roots, and acorns twice boiled, combined in unsalted gruel with bran, straw and an occasional fish," unappetizing. Surprisingly, no one died that winter.

On the morning of July 19, 1629, the white sails of three ships were spotted off the Ile d'Orléans. They anchored off Quebec, just out of range of cannon fire. A small boat was lowered and, flying a white flag, it headed for the colony. An English officer came ashore to meet Champlain. Removing their great beaver hats and bowing deeply, the two men, neither able to speak the other's language, greeted each other civilly. The officer gave Champlain a letter, this time from David Kirke's brothers, Louis and Thomas. Again, they invited Champlain to surrender. This time Champlain had no choice but to accept the English terms. The settlers could take their own possessions and one beaver skin each. They would be guaranteed safe passage to England. From there they would be able to make their way back to France.

The Kirkes took possession of Quebec for England on July 20, 1629. They treated Champlain and the now bed-ridden Pont-Gravé with great courtesy and respect. Both Frenchmen had known the Kirkes' father in Dieppe; the Kirkes were half French, and while growing up in Dieppe they had heard many stories praising the two seasoned explorers.

The new commander of Quebec, Louis Kirke, tore down the French coat of arms from the fortress. In its place he nailed the emblem of England. The English flag flew overhead.

Champlain waited for a ship to take him to England, away from the colony he loved. The days of waiting were filled with sorrow. Among the occupiers he found familiar faces, including Etienne Brûlé and Nicolas Marsolet. The two boys he had brought out in 1608 were now men, and traitors! They had survived that first terrible winter and become the finest of interpreters, only to sell out their honour and Champlain's colony to the English. Kirke invited Louis Hébert's widow and son-in-law to stay on their farm. Champlain advised them to accept the offer.

The voyage to England began on July 24. Champlain must have felt his dreams dying as he watched the tiny colony, his home for twenty years, slowly falling further behind. He watched his English captors ram and seize a French ship on its way — too late — to relieve Quebec. Summer's end found the convoy leaving Tadoussac for England. They arrived in Plymouth to learn that a peace treaty between France and England had been signed in April, *before* the Kirkes had taken Quebec. The capture of the colony had been illegal!

# The Final Voyage Chapter 10

Following the fall of Quebec, Champlain spent three years in France. After two and a half years of negotiations, the Treaty of Saint-Germain-en-Laye was signed on May 29, 1632. Under the terms of the treaty, England handed Quebec back to France. In return, the king of England received a wedding dowry of 400 000 livres from the king of France. Meanwhile, since Hélène had not yet finally decided to enter a convent, Champlain stayed with her in the house in the Rue de la Marche. It was not an easy time for them. There were no more long, sightseeing walks through Paris; the excited talk of life in the New World was a thing of the past. Champlain was now in his mid-sixties while Hélène was still a young woman in her thirties, bitter at a husbandless, childless marriage. Champlain had to acknowledge that their marriage had failed.

*This statue honouring Champlain and his native guides stands in Ottawa*

The three years spent in Paris were busy ones. Champlain passionately continued to promote the idea of a permanent French settlement in North America. Much of his time was spent trying to win the support of the king and Cardinal Richelieu. There were also meetings with the directors of the Company of One Hundred Associates. Champlain reminded them that England and Holland had set up farming colonies to the south of New France. The colonies were well established and growing stronger all the time. The English and Dutch controlled the fur trade with the Iroquois and were arming the Indians for their wars against the Huron, the allies of the French. Champlain told them that it would only be a matter of time before the Quebec colony would come under attack again, either from the English or their Indian allies. He urged French leaders to support and defend New France; without this support, the colony could not survive.

With the signing of the treaty, the company sent a party of settlers to reclaim Quebec. When they arrived, the Kirkes surrendered the colony. It had deteriorated badly in English hands. The *habitation* that Champlain had built twenty-five years before had been burned to

*This detail, enlarged from the picture on page 36, is Champlain's only known drawing of himself*

the ground. The French settlers who had remained at Quebec were living in fear. English traders had given the local Indians brandy in exchange for furs, with the result that there were drunken parties and fights nearly every night. Murder had become commonplace.

In France, unaware of the condition of the French colony, Champlain was busy putting the finishing touches to his latest book, the *Voyages*, published in 1632. The old explorer saw it as the crowning glory of his long career. On its title page, he proclaims France's right to North America by virtue of discovery and settlement. In the text, he presents a solemn message to France about her glorious opportunities in the New World, spelling out the steps to be taken and pitfalls to be avoided. The text is full of glowing descriptions of New France and the great riches that it holds. Champlain included in the book a masterpiece of his craft as a cartographer, the largest and most up-to-date map of the region yet produced.

In the fall, ships returned to France from Quebec. Champlain listened eagerly to the news from the colony. What he heard shocked him. It was obvious that he was needed to set things right again. During the winter he made plans and preparations. The Company of One Hundred Associates was fitting out three ships to go to Quebec the following spring. For the first time Champlain was to be in complete command of the settlement on the St. Lawrence.

The colony leader was warmly welcomed back to the territory he had left almost four year earlier. Jesuit priests brought a choir of young Indian boys, students at a Jesuit school, aboard Champlain's pinnace. There they sang the Lord's Prayer translated into their own language.

Champlain quickly set about putting the battered colony in order. Throughout the summer the men worked to build a new *habitation* and a new warehouse. Champlain fulfilled his promise to build a church if Quebec was restored to the French.

Recognizing the damage strong drink was doing to the Indian way of life, one of Champlain's first acts on his return to Quebec was to issue an order prohibiting the sale or gift of liquor to the Indians. Any Frenchman found breaking the order would be severely punished.

That summer of 1633, the Huron broke through the Iroquois blockade of the St. Lawrence. They brought a rich cargo of furs to trade. They also brought news, an open secret that was soon whispered from ear to ear throughout the colony. Etienne Brûlé, Champlain's interpreter turned traitor, had been killed during the winter. After a quarrel, perhaps over suspicions of betrayal to the English, he had been killed by the Huron and then ceremonially eaten. The Huron were afraid that the French might seek to avenge Brûlé's death. Champlain quickly assured them that Brûlé had lost any claim to being a French citizen when he betrayed the colony to the English.

In the spring of 1634 Champlain was content. The colony was flourishing at last. A steady stream of new settlers cleared and farmed the land. There would be no more hungry winters of the kind Champlain had endured too often.

There were also some regrets. Peace had not yet been made with the Iroquois; it seemed it never would be. Champlain urged the king of France to send an army to defeat the Iroquois soundly and thus assure the colony's future. Relations were good with the Huron, the Algonquin and the Montagnais. Twice, in his speeches to the yearly fur-trade banquets, Champlain called for marriage between Indians and French, saying, "Our young men shall marry your daughters and we shall be one people." But the Jesuits were having little success with their mission. Only a few baptisms were being performed each year, usually of young children on their deathbeds.

Perhaps the biggest failure of all was the fact that Champlain had not yet reached the Pacific Ocean that he had seen once, more than thirty years earlier, in Panama. The dream of reaching the Pacific and finding a route to China was still with him. For many years his favourite interpreter, Jean Nicolet, had carried a cloak of Chinese silk damask in his bag. It was there for that day when the dream would come true.

But time was running out for the old explorer. He was now nearing seventy. In the fall of 1635 a paralyzing stroke confined him to his bed in the governor's chamber of the fort. From his window he watched fall turn to winter. One midnight, a cannon was fired at the fort. Champlain heard the shot boom and echo, announcing the arrival of Christmas Day, 1635. The Quebec colonists had gathered for midnight mass in the little church of Notre Dame de la Recouvrance.

Lying in bed, Champlain listened to the congregation sing the *Te Deum Laudemus*. Inside the church, prayers were said for the health of the colony's leader. As the songs of joy and praise faded away in the cold night air, the great captain's strength failed him at last. Champlain received the last rites of the church from the priest and died as the day dawned. His death came exactly one hundred years after Cartier and his men had celebrated the first French Christmas at Quebec.

The tiny community deeply mourned the loss of its leader. A procession of priests, officers, soldiers and colonists walked behind the body as it was carried to the church. The Jesuit priest, Père LeJeune, gave the funeral oration. It was a simple speech about a man whose life spoke for itself; "On the 25th of December, the day of the birth of our Saviour on earth, Monsieur de Champlain was reborn in Heaven." Champlain was buried beneath the floor of the church of Notre Dame de la Recouvrance. A chapel was built over his grave to honour the memory of the founder of Quebec.

Champlain's Indian allies were as deeply moved by his death as the Quebec colonists. At the spring fur trade in 1636, the Huron brought with them a fine collection of wampum pelts. These they gave to the French colonists in memory of the dead Champlain. "They are given," said a Huron leader, "To help you wipe away your tears."

Champlain's death went almost unnoticed in his native land. In fact, it spared him the pain of knowing that an ungrateful France no longer desired his services. Unknown to him, he had already been replaced as Cardinal Richelieu's lieutenant in Canada. His replacement, Charles de Montmagny, arrived in the spring of 1636, having left France before word of Champlain's death had crossed the Atlantic. He carried with him not a word of thanks from either the king or cardinal for Champlain's thirty years of work in Canada. As a further insult, Montmagny had been named governor of New France. It was a title Champlain had never enjoyed, despite the many years he had served in

that role.

Champlain had lived to see the struggling colony establish itself as a permanent settlement, but his dream of founding a secure, prosperous French dominion in North America with its capital at Quebec was not fulfilled in his lifetime. Champlain knew that a strong commitment to Canada from France was needed for the colony to match the strength and growth of the English colonies to the south. Just before his death, Champlain sent a moving letter to Cardinal Richelieu:

*Quebec in 1640
Champlain lived to see the habitation he had established as a trading centre at Quebec grow into a flourishing permanent settlement.*

This country is so great that it stretches out more than 4000 km. In it is one of the best rivers in the world into which many other rivers empty themselves. These rivers grace a countryside in which many different people live. Some are wandering hunters or fishermen; others are farmers who live in villages with houses made of wood. The beauty of these lands cannot be overpraised for the fertility of the soil, the extent of the forests, and the opportunities for hunting and fishing in abundance.

All these things hold out their arms to you, Monseigneur. It seems that God had reserved these lands for you. You may bring forward from them a progress pleasing to Him, more than anyone else before you has.

Monseigneur, please pardon my zeal. Your fame has now reached the Orient. It should be better known in the New World. . . .

Champlain had struggled to realize his dream for thirty-two years, and it was still strong in his heart when he died. The leaders and rulers back in France failed to listen to the advice of the "Father of New France," and the French eventually lost all of their colonies in North America to the British. But Champlain's dream of flourishing French settlement has been realized. Today, Samuel de Champlain is remembered proudly as a founder of Quebec, and of Canada.

# Further Reading

Bishop, Morris. *Champlain, The Life of Fortitude* Toronto: McClelland & Stewart, 1963

Champlain, Samuel de. *Voyages to New France* Ottawa: Oberon, 1970

Garrod, S. and Neering, R. *Life in New France* Toronto: Fitzhenry & Whiteside, 1976

Grant, Matthew G. *Champlain* Minneapolis: Creative Education, 1974

Jacobs, William. *Samuel de Champlain* New York: Watts, 1974

Morison, Samuel E. *Samuel de Champlain, Father of New France* New York: Little, 1972

Trudel, Marcel *The Beginnings of New France* 1524-1663 Toronto: McClelland & Stewart, 1973

Windsor, Kenneth. *Champlain* Canadian Jackdaws Series. Toronto: Clarke, Irwin.

# Credits

Champlain Society, page 45

Champlain Society and Toronto Metro Library, pages 5, 9, 10, 11, 15, 18, 20, 22, 25, 27, 33, 36, 47, 50, 60

Department of Indian Affairs, page 38

National Capital Commission, page 59 and cover

Public Archives of Canada, pages 4 (C-2921), 6(C-69191), 29(C-73557), 34(C-11075), 39(C-73448), 42(C-73632), 49(C-2007), 55(C-6643), 56(C-73635), 63(C-6492), title page and cover

# Index